KIRIGAMI

EXQUISITE PROJECTS TO FOLD AND CUT

JEFFREY RUTZKY

METRO BOOKS

NEW YORK

This 2007 edition published by Metro Books,
by arrangement with Quirk Packaging, Inc.

Written, designed, and diagrammed by
Jeffrey Rutzky
Edited by Tricia Levi
Photographs by Mark A. Gore

Metro Books
122 Fifth Avenue
New York, New York 10011

ISBN-13: 978-0-7607-9227-8

Printed and bound in China

10 9 8 7 6 5 4 3 2

ACKNOWLEDGMENTS

Thank you to all of the creators who generously
gave permission for many of the designs in this
book. I encourage you to build upon their work
and techniques to develop many more creations.

Kirigami is my third papercraft book. *Jewelgami*
and *Bugagami* are titles in the unique Tear-I-Gami
series of origami books, available from Barnes &
Noble, Inc. Thank you to everyone who enjoys
these books!

Thanks to Lynne Yeamans who art directed
the book and packaging, Mark A. Gore who
professionally photographed the models I crafted,
and Tricia Levi for overseeing the project and for
being a great editor. I am grateful to the staff of
Quirk Packaging and to Devorah Klein at Barnes
& Noble, Inc., who created many of the models
to be certain you can too. However, I am always
most grateful to Sharyn Rosart and Nathaniel
Marunas for their support and encouragement,
and for entrusting me to expand my creativity
by sharing it with others.

Several paper engineers were very helpful when
I began to write and design this book: Masahiro
Chatani, Chris Palmer, Paul Jackson, and
Florence Temko have not only been contributors,
but were inspirational by taking paper-based
art further in so many ways. My wife, Nanci,
continues to contribute greatly to my publishing
and production efforts.

The models in this book were selected to
reflect a broad range of ways art can be made
from cutting paper. All of the tools used in this
book were purchased at local craft supply stores.
The paper used to make the models pictured
was purchased at local paper specialty stores
(see Artists' Resources on pages 106).

The designs in this book are intended for
personal use. Commercial use of any original
model, in print or other media, requires the permission of the individual creator. The publishers
have made every reasonable effort to contact the
creators of the models herein. We apologize for
any omissions and would be pleased to correct
any such omissions in subsequent editions of
this work. Please write to: Kirigami Editor,
Quirk Packaging, Inc., 55 Washington Street,
Suite 804, Brooklyn, New York 11201.

To my wife Nanci:
Like snow, falling paper scraps—
We sweep, and love grows.

INTRODUCTION

What Is Kirigami?....................................6
The History of Paper Cutting..................6
What Kinds of Paper Should I Use? 7
What Tools Do I Need?............................8
What Is All This Stuff?...........................8
Folding the Paper Before You Cut 10
Symmetry from Folding.........................11
Pop-Ups, Up-Pops, and Cutaways 12
Scoring, Creasing, and Cutting...............12
Sharpening Your Scissor Skills................13
Honing Your X-Acto Handling 14
Imperial to Metric Conversions..............15
Half, Square, & Spider Folds 16
Snowflake Fold 17
Starburst Fold 18
Pleated Fold 19

EASY PROJECTS ANYONE CAN CUT

Classic Snowflake 22
Dendritic Snowflake 23
Spider Web 24
Spiders Everywhere................................25
Elephant Frame.....................................26
Airplane Hangar....................................27
Valentine Heartflake..............................28
Cupid's Arrow.......................................29
Tulip Hearts...30
Sunshine Star 31
Celtic Cross 32
Celtic Knot 33
French Filigree Doily..............................34
Quilty Doily..35
Papel Picado Pájaros..............................36
3-D Christmas Ornament........................37
Bell Net 38
Decorative Orbs & Garland.....................39
Kirigami Alphabet 40
Quickiri Booklet....................................46

CUTTING INTO ANOTHER DIMENSION

3-D Snowflake 50
3-D Lucky Clover..................................51
Heartfelt Pop-Up Card 52
Cupid's Arrow Pop-Up Card...................53

Concentric Squares................................54
Concentric Circles.................................55
Tetra Perpetual Calendar........................56
Trillium Up-Pop Card.............................57
Making a Mobile 58
Cutaway Blinds 59
Clever Cube 60
Plover Greeting Card..............................61
Polar Light 62
Slide-together.......................................63

HOW TO BE A PAPER ARCHITECT

Introduction 66
0°, 90°, 180°, and 360° 66
Enlarge, Transfer, and Cut the Pattern.....67
Flex, Fold, and Flatten...........................67
Making a Backing Card, if Desired...........67
Generation Half-Steps............................68
Cargo Ship...69
Sunset on the Sea 70
Cancer the Crab 71
Chatani Castle.......................................72
Modern Tower 73
Empire State Building.............................74
Statue of Liberty 75
Modern Temple 76
Erechtheion 77
Green Apple 78
Rialto Bridge 80
Wind Gauge Book..................................81

PATTERNS AND ARTIST'S RESOURCES

Patterns.:..83
Artist's Resources..................................105
About the Author...................................112

INTRODUCTION TO KIRIGAMI

What Is Kirigami?

Most of us are familiar with origami, the ancient art of paper folding. But when you cut paper into decorative forms, the Japanese call it *monkiri* (mon-kee-ree). Kirigami was increasingly popularized by American author Florence Temko in the 1960s. *Kiri* means "cutting," and *gami* means "paper." Origami is still used to make kirigami. *Ori* means "folding," and there are different folding steps to layer the paper before cutting begins. Origami techniques may also be used after cutting to make three-dimensional works, as in origamic architecture.

Paper cutting can take many forms: a simple snowflake, a string of paper dolls, or a length of garland; abstract sculpture, pop-up cards, and intricate paper architecture. Sometimes all you need are a sharp pair of scissors and a piece of paper. Other forms require precision X-Acto knife cuts, cardstock, and glue.

The History of Paper Cutting

Paper cutting has its roots in many different cultures, beginning with the invention of modern paper made with wood pulp by the Chinese. They began cutting designs, known as *chien-chih* (**jian**-jeh), depicting numerous themes, including the Chinese zodiac and "window flowers." Many Chinese designs are scenic and made without folding. In the countryside, girls were expected to master the craft. Men formed workgroups to make templates for elaborate patterns on porcelain and textiles.

Origami and paper cutting didn't reach Japan until about the sixth century AD.

JIACAI YIN

Senga is another form of traditional Japanese paper cutting. Detailed scenes are cut from black washi paper and then pasted onto white washi paper. Often the scene is decorated with watercolor paints, adding brilliant colors within the cutout spaces.

However, it took another millennium for the paper-cut art forms we are familiar with today to reach Europe. By the seventeenth century, different paper-cut crafts had spread quickly throughout the world.

In Poland, the art of *wycinanki* (vee-chee-**non**-kee), or "scissors cutting," has been handed down from generation to generation by farmers' wives. Cuttings often depict rural life. Wycinanki artists historically use sheep shears as long as twelve inches! The layering of paper is also used to detail more colors or asymmetrical designs.

German and Swiss paper cutters call their form *scherenschnitte* (sher-en-**shnit**-uh), which also means "scissors cutting." The art of silhouette cutting became popular as travelers very experienced in paper cutting cut likenesses of families and village countrysides.

SELF-PORTRAIT BY GERLOF SMIT

Compared to a painting, silhouettes were an inexpensive form of portraiture. One outstanding artist, Gerlof Smit, cut likenesses of his entire village in The Netherlands. Europeans also began folding the paper first, thus cutting through layers that formed symmetrical patterns. In France, paper cutting is called *canivet*, which means "little knife."

Still another style, called *papel picado*, literally "punched paper," dates back to pre-Columbian times in Mexico. Patterns were made by hammering differently shaped punches through many layers of colored tissue paper. Banners often commemorated traditional holidays and fiestas. Scissors and X-Acto knives are now used more widely than the punches.

In this book we'll create a variety of projects using paper, scissors, X-Acto knives, special punches, gluing, and folding, so you can contribute your creations to this art form with its rich and diverse history.

Throughout this introduction, and at the end of each chapter, are photos of some traditional examples of kirigami from around the world, as well as some outstanding examples of modern designs.

Apologies to readers who use metric measurements; please see the chart on page 15 for the most common conversions required to make the models in this book.

WHAT KINDS OF PAPER SHOULD I USE?

Some models will require thinner paper to facilitate cutting through many layers at a time; other models need heavier papers or cardstocks to maintain their shape and structure. With those basic requirements in mind, you can still choose from a huge variety of stocks—even plastics!

Most of the delicate kirigami and paper-cut models can be made with the paper samples that come with this book. These are *kami* weight, and are often sold simply labeled as origami paper. Papers of a similar weight include most gift wrap and magazine interiors. Resist the urge to tear open a gift wrapped with exquisite paper; tear out beautifully designed magazine pages with photographs of textures that you like. Flat kirigami can be displayed in a frame or glued to another background, so the other side won't show in the final art.

Tissue papers come in a myriad of colors and printed textures. Although much more fragile, these weights can be helpful when cutting intricate shapes or many layers at once.

Thin acetates, mylars, and other plastics can be used creatively. Their translucency is particularly appealing when making window ornaments.

Some of the designs pictured in this book have been made using translucent vellum. There are a few different weights and often many colors to choose from. Paper vellum is not suitable for kirigami paper cutting, and will crack if folded more than once in the same place. However, its appeal for sculptural models is hard to resist. Use these papers once you're proficient at precise cutting and folding since they also show every little unintentional bend or overcut.

Pop-ups, origamic architecture, and other paper sculptures benefit from a sturdier material. Regular card or cover stock, sold in every office supply store, is sufficient for all of these models. Most stores stock at least a few colors, and some can be inkjet- or laser-printed with your own designs or pictures before you cut. (A tip about at-home printing: Don't use glossy "premium" photo papers because these contain plastic on the surface that will crack when folded. Premium matte cardstocks are ideal!)

Paper specialty stores have cardstocks that come in many weights, as well as beautiful styles and patterns. Textured, often handmade papers give a very rich look to greeting cards and sculptural models. Some papers contain "inclusions": silk, real flower petals, grains, bits of metallic flakes, and even paper-thin dried fruits! These papers might work, but often just where you need to fold or cut, something is in the way. Use caution when planning a model with these types of paper. It's worth noting that esoteric papers can still make great backgrounds for greeting cards or thin kirigami creations. Read the section "Scoring, Creasing, and Cutting" on pages 12–13 to determine how grain direction and other factors will affect folding your models.

There are many clear and colored plastic materials that make great models. Polypropylene envelopes, organizers, or even sheet protectors work well. Experiment with different thicknesses and types; some tend to crack when folded, especially if you want the model to fold over and over again. Read the section "Honing Your X-Acto Handling" on pages 14–15 because plastic can be slippery and thus hard to cut.

One last consideration: paper longevity. Inexpensive paper and cardstock may not be pH neutral, acid free, or archival. For most creations you may not care if the design will be perfectly preserved for twenty years—or even five. But if you spend a lot of time and effort cutting, folding, gluing, and maybe framing something spectacular, then paying attention to this hidden detail is worthwhile. When giving a gift that someone will treasure forever, how best to prevent it from fading or cracking has to be a decision made before you start.

What Tools Do I Need?

To create most of the designs in this book the simple answer is: a small pair of sharp scissors. A more thorough answer, however, will vary from project to project. Each project will describe the tools necessary to achieve the best possible outcome. Some projects using cardstocks will require scoring before folding, making precise cuts, and taping or gluing pieces together. There are many hand punches with standard shapes such as circles, stars, and hearts. These tools can embellish small areas of multilayered paper that would be almost impossible to cut with scissors or an X-Acto knife.

Tools can include:

> - A small pair of sharp scissors with narrow blades
> - An X-Acto knife (preferably with #11 blade—and lots of them!)
> - A steel ruler with a non-slip, cork underside
> - Cutting mat
> - A #12 or #14 (1 mm or 0.75 mm) crochet needle for scoring or a stylus
> - Glue suitable for paper-to-paper bonds
> - Pushpin
> - Long-handled, thin tweezers
> - $\frac{1}{16}$-inch hole punch
> - Photocopier with percentage enlargement or scanner and printer
> - Protractor

What Is All This Stuff?

Scissors

The secret to scissor success: think small and sharp. Scissors can be found at many craft stores, discount pharmacies, or department stores. Straight-blade manicure scissors work well, but the curve-blade ones won't. After some trial-and-error experience, you may find that the best little scissors are on the Victorinox "Swiss Army" Classic knife. The scissors are strong and very sharp. The small knife blade is even good to make the "starter" slit for cutouts that would be difficult to complete solely with an X-Acto. Even the nail file has a dull "screwdriver" end that's

perfect for scoring. One caveat: beware of knockoffs. Only the Victorinox's scissors are made well enough to work with many layers of paper and to cut intricate designs precisely. Surgical scissors also work well. Tips and techniques for using scissors are in "Sharpening Your Scissor Skills" on pages 13–14.

X-Acto Knife

X-Acto knives are the best for cutting paper. A #11 blade is the most common and is very pointy on the end. This is preferable to other hobby knives that tend to have broader points. It's very important to use these knives against a steel ruler, held securely above the blade. Change your blade often; a dull blade will drag and tear the paper. Never cut in the direction of your hands. All hobby knives are razor sharp! Tips and techniques for using X-Acto knives are in "Honing Your X-Acto Handling" on pages 14–15.

Steel Ruler

A steel ruler with a non-slip, cork underside is required for any hobby knife use. The non-slip underside is crucial when making a series of precise cuts along a virtually invisible line. If the rule slips even one millimeter, the project could be ruined. Never use a wood or plastic ruler to cut against. The blade can easily "jump" the edge. Some wood rulers have thin metal edges embedded in them; however, it is worth investing in a steel ruler that will last a lifetime. Tips and techniques for using steel rulers are in "Scoring, Creasing, and Cutting" on pages 12–13.

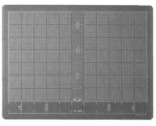

Cutting Mat

Cutting mats, also known as "self-healing mats," are a great surface to cut on. Blades will last longer and there's less risk of that precious tabletop getting scratched.

Crochet Needle for Scoring

A #12 or #14 (1 mm or 0.75 mm) crochet needle is valuable for scoring against your steel ruler. Other options are a stylus, an inkless ballpoint pen, or a bonefolder (bookbinder's tool). Tips and techniques for using steel rulers are in "Scoring, Creasing, and Cutting" on pages 12–13.

Glue

Paper glues are as familiar as standard white glue, but they also come in convenient glue sticks. White glue should be used sparingly because too much can soak and deform the paper.  Spray-type glue is essential for mounting kirigami papercuts to backgrounds. It's nearly impossible to spread liquid glue or draw a glue stick against the delicate cut edges. Use light-tack spray-type glue in a well-ventilated area. Only a quick spray is necessary to adhere the lightweight paper cut; be careful the propellant itself doesn't move the art into an area where overspray will mar the front side. Place wax paper on top of the positioned art and smooth down any edges with your hands; don't use a roller or brayer since it may wrinkle the art. Double-sided tape is handy for tacking down flaps without glue. It's generally not as strong as paper glue, but for most lightweight papers and cardstocks it can be very convenient. Be sure to get the "permanent" kind.

Pushpin
A good, sharp pushpin will be handy for transferring designs to cardstocks for scoring and cutting references. This is the most commonly used method when making origamic architecture models. Try to get the all-metal variety since these tend to have the sharpest points. A hatpin or a compass needle will also work.

Long-handled, Thin Tweezers

Tweezers aid in carefully pulling or pushing small parts forward or backward in an intricate origamic architecture model. Sometimes the fold line is only ⅛-inch long and using your fingers may tear the fragile form.

Photocopier or Scanner and Printer
Many of the patterns in this book will be a percentage of the final size to transfer to your paper. Use a photocopier with a percent-adjustable enlargement setting to make a copy at the correct working size of the model. Using a scanner can be even more valuable! With a few desktop publishing skills, you can print the patterns at any size, or even onto the working paper itself. It might be easier to print patterns on inexpensive cardstocks, complete with cut-and-fold lines, before committing the final version using the pushpin method on a valuable piece of material. Another advantage with scanning is you can use software to change the lines to a very light gray or yellow and print a reversed pattern directly onto the back of the final material. Depending on how you are displaying the

model, sometimes the back won't show, or the light-colored lines may be nearly undetectable.

Protractor
Traditional kirigami is cut after a square of paper is pre-folded a number of times. The angle you fold around the center point determines whether you have two-, four-, five-, six-, eight-, or even ten-fold symmetry. There are guidelines printed with the Snowflake and Starburst folds (pages 17–18) to aid in folding your paper to the proper angles. The protractor is still a valuable tool when making pop-ups since certain angles must be equal so the card will fold flat.

FOLDING THE PAPER BEFORE YOU CUT

Valley Folds and Mountain Folds
Nearly all of the projects have some folds: pre-folds for kirigami paper cuts, folds that make three-dimensional shapes, or folds that act as hinges.

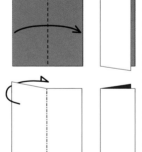

A Valley Fold will fold toward the front and is shown with a *dashed* line. A Mountain Fold will fold toward the back and is shown with a *dash-dot* line. An arrowhead showing a Valley Fold will be *solid* whereas an arrowhead for a Mountain Fold will be *hollow*. These are the same conventions used in origami diagrams. *For additional clarity on smaller fold lines in the Origamic Architecture chapter, Valley Folds are shown in red, and Mountain Folds are shown in blue.*

This section also gives you tips on folding thin paper for kirigami paper cuts, garlands, chains, and nets. For help folding cardstocks when making greeting cards, pop-ups, and other three-dimensional models, see "Scoring, Creasing, and Cutting" on pages 12–13.

Most designs use symmetry to create beautiful patterns. Often you'll never know how nice a kirigami design will look until you've made a few cuts into neatly folded layers of paper—and then, almost magically, a striking design appears—or the paper simply falls to pieces because there were too many cuts!

Rule Number One

Neatness counts. A lot! Most of the kirigami designs, including a simple alphabet, will be folded from a square. Depending on how many times and at what angles you fold, the result may be a frame or border, pentagonal leaf, or a hexagonal snowflake. Most of us have cut paper dolls or other streamers from pleated paper, but we've also made snowflakes that are eight-sided! This is because it's easier to fold the paper using forty-five degree angles instead of measuring accurately to get sixty-degree angles— the true structure of real snowflakes.

Making the Pre-fold

Each kirigami paper-cut model will tell you what pre-fold to start with. There are simple Half and Pleated folds that give mirror images of what you cut. Fold the Half Fold again and you've got the Square Fold—this will make frames and borders. Fold the Square Fold in half again diagonally and you've got the Spider Fold. (This is one of the most common folds, giving you eight layers to cut through, but it's also the one that is most mistakenly used when cutting snowflakes.)

The more difficult pre-folds are the Snowflake and Starburst folds. Snowflake Folds give you six layers, or even twelve if you double-back the folds. Starburst Folds will make ten layers, and are often used when pentagonal symmetry is desired, such as for stars and leaves. For these pre-folds, there are guides printed on the page to line up the paper; this makes using a protractor unnecessary.

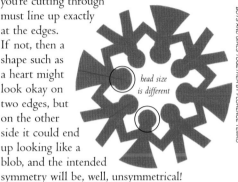

The reason neatness counts so much when pre-folding is because all of the layers you're cutting through must line up exactly at the edges. If not, then a shape such as a heart might look okay on two edges, but on the other side it could end up looking like a blob, and the intended symmetry will be, well, unsymmetrical!

head size is different

SYMMETRY FROM FOLDING

The axis of symmetry comes from how many times you fold the paper, and at which angle the folds radiate from the center of the kirigami. It's helpful to have some knowledge about how different angles will make basic shapes—without getting into a full-blown geometry lesson.

The Half Fold—just folding the paper in half— is the simplest and historically most used. Except for snowflake folding, most paper cutters don't pre-fold their designs along more than one axis of symmetry, although you can have parallel axes of symmetry in a Pleated Fold.

The Square Fold has two perpendicular axes of symmetry, either diagonal or parallel to the edges of the paper. Four fold lines are ninety degrees from one another.

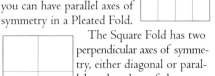

The Spider Fold has four axes of symmetry, both diagonal and parallel to the edges of the paper. Eight fold lines are forty-five degrees from one another.

The Snowflake Fold has three axes of symmetry. Six fold lines are sixty degrees from one another. The Angle Set Fold is sixty degrees from the base fold line.

The Starburst Fold has five axes of symmetry. Ten fold lines are thirty-six degrees from one another. This fold is a little more confusing: the Angle Set

Fold is seventy-two degrees from the base fold line; doubling back these folds bisects the angle to thirty-six degrees.

It's possible with tissue paper to fold an increasingly narrow wedge with more folded edges to cut from, but the thickness from so many layers of paper combines with another problem: paper slippage. Hints to avoid the paper slipping out of alignment are discussed in "Sharpening Your Scissor Skills" on pages 13–14.

POP-UPS, UP-POPS, AND CUTAWAYS

What's the Difference Between a Pop-Up and an Up-Pop?

A pop-up can take many forms. Just a simple folded notch in the middle of a card can suggest a nose or mouth—glue a panel on one side and it will wave to and fro. Complex scenes use a variety of tabs and slits, all folded and glued in just the right places. The kinetic energy you exert by opening and closing make the mechanisms come to life.

An up-pop, on the other hand, uses a "stored energy" mechanism, such as a stretched rubber band. Its surprise lies dormant, hidden inside an envelope, waiting

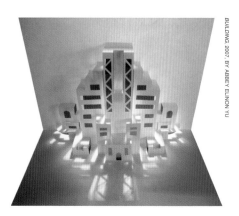

BUILDING 2007, BY ABBEY ELINON YU

for you to open it; that's when it snaps to life. The model can take the shape of a container, swing something out at you, or even bite!

What's a Cutaway?

Origamic architecture has its foundation in the cutaway. A series of slits and folds can describe a simple abstract paper sculpture or a detailed rendering of a building. Artists have, in fact, made pop-up façades of nearly every famous architectural landmark in the world.

Made from a single sheet of cardstock, there's relatively little assembly compared to pop-ups. But with cutaways it can be very tricky to get each part to fold the right way—and the more detailed the piece, the more fragile it becomes. The dramatic effect that light and shadow can play, and the seemingly impossible structures that arise from a myriad of cuts and folds, make it worthwhile to create these works of art.

SCORING, CREASING, AND CUTTING

Handmade paper folds differently from machine-made—and machine-made papers have another wrinkle—grain!

What Is Grain?

The fibers used in machine-made papers and cardstocks run parallel to the sides of the sheet. Which side? Does it matter? The thicker the cardstock, the more it matters, and the key is to take advantage of each paper's properties when preparing a model. To avoid getting too technical, just keep these hints in mind: thin cardstock folds perpendicular to the grain; thick cardstock folds parallel to the grain. This will become more obvious as you practice scoring and creasing different stocks.

But How Do I Tell What Direction the Grain Is?

This is fairly easy with thicker cardstocks. Cut out any size square and fold it in half; then fold it in half the other way. One crease will be smooth and one will be, well, not-so-smooth. The grain runs in the direction of the smooth crease. The majority of each model's folds should take advantage of this property. For thinner stocks, making the folds perpendicular to the grain will make the models stiffer and stand up better. On thicker stocks, creasing parallel to the grain makes neater lines.

For text-weight and thin paper this whole grain business doesn't matter much at all.

Ruler Set? Score!

Folding thick or thin cardstock is infinitely easier if it's scored first. In fact, it's required for most of the pop-up and origamic architecture models in this book. Use a #12 crochet needle or stylus with a small, smooth point and a steel ruler—connect the dots and press firmly along the length. Make the score along a crease that's valley-folded; for Mountain Folds on the

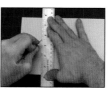

same side, just flip the card over before you start scoring.

Scoring the models carefully can mean the difference between the effortless building of your architecture or fighting to flip that errant flap into place.

SHARPENING YOUR SCISSOR SKILLS

Scissors are the primary, and often the only, tool used to create paper cuts. When cutting more intricate kirigami pieces, a knife or punch will help "start" an interior cut, but scissors can be used to make all of the thin-paper models in this book. Since using scissors is such a large part of kirigami, there are a few tips and techniques discussed here that will make your paper cuts accurate, as well as help keep your fingers safe.

Sharp Scissors Shape Safely

After you've invested in a small, narrow-bladed set of scissors, it's important to keep them sharp. Use these paper-craft scissors for cutting only one thing: thin paper! For cardstocks used with other models, an X-Acto or a larger pair of sharp scissors should be used. Many precision scissors are somewhat self-sharpening, since the blades scrape each other uniformly. Paper contains chemicals that eventually wear down the edges, but miles of cuts may be made before this happens.

Cut On the Right Side of the Line

Or left side, if you're left-handed and have lefty scissors. Most of us lefties have

adapted to using right-handed scissors, so make sure your new pair has a universal handle. The important thing is to be able to see the line clearly, with an unobstructed view of what lies ahead to be cut. This means that the right blade is above the paper and the left blade below.

Short, Slow, Tight, and Steady

Precision will be greatest when cutting close to the fulcrum of the scissors. Keep the paper tight against the crossing blades so that you can "feel" the cut dividing the paper. This is also where the least effort is required to make cuts through many layers. Avoid finishing the cut with a closing snap of the blades; slow and steady scissor movements result in less error. The blades always tend to slide the layers out of alignment, so another reason to keep the cuts short, slow, tight, and steady is so you can hold the layers of paper more securely. Unless you opt for the Swiss Army knife's tiny scissors, never use the first 50 percent of the blade length at all.

Scissor Straight Through the Curve

Get used to turning the paper rather than moving your scissor-holding hand. It's much easier to guide the paper into the blades than cutting outward. Practice will help you learn how much hand versus paper movement is necessary for a particular cut.

Scissoring Safely

Since safety scissors aren't practical for kirigami, except for simple snowflakes, scissoring safely will keep your fingers out of harm's way. Lucky if you're a lefty and your right hand is gripping the paper (if cutting on the right side of the line), it will be opposite the view of the work. But most paper cutters will be gripping the paper with their left hand, and fairly close to the scissor blades—yet another reason for Short, Slow, Tight, and Steady cutting: safety!

HONING YOUR X-ACTO HANDLING

Nearly every paper-craft person working with razor-sharp knives has an X-Acto accident story you won't want to happen to you. Using a good, cork-backed steel ruler and fresh blades are key in not cutting yourself. Experience will lead to dexterity too.

Keep the Other Hand "Above" the Cut

When holding the steel ruler, position your hand above the beginning of the cut. If the cut is more than about five inches, stop cutting so you can slide your hand down to maintain pressure on the steel ruler, then continue cutting. Experience will help you to know how much to cut at a time. But the key to a precise cut is not having the steel ruler slip. Steel rulers are essential for making straight cuts, but when making freehand curved cuts, sharp blades will be helpful to a steady hand. Again, keep the other hand above where you're cutting. Never cut toward your hand.

Cut Your Way from the Inside Out

Plan the cutting of your model so the shapes closer to the center are cut first. Cut small shapes next. More paper to hold helps to stabilize cutting and prevent dragging previous cuts. Turn the paper to take advantage of cutting in a direction that does not "pull" on the most delicate areas.

Cutting Curves and Corners

When cutting freehand curves, use the same technique as with the scissors: rotate the paper, keeping the knife straight. It takes some practice, but the ideal cut is achieved by not lifting the blade—making an uninterrupted, continuous curve.

Don't cut corners cutting corners! Corner and pointy cuts can be made neatly if both cuts leading to the corner's point are made in the same direction. Cut toward the corner until you reach the point; finish cutting to the corner on its other side. This way a small point won't be dragged or damaged by the knife.

Measure Twice, Cut Twice?

Measuring twice is a good practice. Thicker cardstocks are best cut with two or sometimes three light strokes along the steel ruler rather than one heavy stroke, intended to cut through the first time. Make sure the ruler doesn't move between cuts. Cutting curves with successive strokes can be very difficult. Don't let "tracking" the first cut give you false confidence to increase speed on the second or third strokes. Again, slow and steady will make the best cut. ✳

IMPERIAL TO METRIC CONVERSIONS

Imperial	Metric	Imperial	Metric
$\frac{1}{16}$ inch	$1\frac{1}{2}$ mm	5 inches	127 mm
$\frac{1}{8}$ inch	3 mm	$5\frac{1}{4}$ inches	133 mm
$\frac{1}{4}$ inch	6 mm	$5\frac{1}{2}$ inches	140 mm
$\frac{3}{8}$ inch	10 mm	$5\frac{3}{4}$ inches	146 mm
$\frac{1}{2}$ inch	13 mm	6 inches	152 mm
$\frac{5}{8}$ inch	16 mm	$6\frac{1}{4}$ inches	159 mm
$\frac{3}{4}$ inch	19 mm	$6\frac{1}{2}$ inches	165 mm
$\frac{7}{8}$ inch	22 mm	$6\frac{3}{4}$ inches	171 mm
1 inch	25 mm	7 inches	178 mm
$1\frac{1}{4}$ inches	32 mm	$7\frac{1}{4}$ inches	184 mm
$1\frac{1}{2}$ inches	38 mm	$7\frac{1}{2}$ inches	191 mm
$1\frac{3}{4}$ inches	44 mm	$7\frac{3}{4}$ inches	197 mm
2 inches	51 mm	8 inches	203 mm
$2\frac{1}{4}$ inches	57 mm	$8\frac{1}{4}$ inches	210 mm
$2\frac{1}{2}$ inches	64 mm	$8\frac{1}{2}$ inches	216 mm
$2\frac{3}{4}$ inches	70 mm	$8\frac{3}{4}$ inches	222 mm
3 inches	76 mm	9 inches	227 mm
$3\frac{1}{4}$ inches	83 mm	$9\frac{1}{4}$ inches	235 mm
$3\frac{1}{2}$ inches	89 mm	$9\frac{1}{2}$ inches	241 mm
$3\frac{3}{4}$ inches	95 mm	$9\frac{3}{4}$ inches	248 mm
4 inches	102 mm	10 inches	254 mm
$4\frac{1}{4}$ inches	108 mm	$10\frac{1}{2}$ inches	267 mm
$4\frac{1}{2}$ inches	114 mm	11 inches	279 mm
$4\frac{3}{4}$ inches	120 mm	12 inches	305 mm

THE ORCHESTRA, 2006, 32" × 16", MULTILAYERED PAPER CUT BY ANNA KRONICK

Half, S

These pre-folds are the simplest ways to get started with kirigami. The Half Fold has only one axis of symmetry. The Square Fold has two perpendicular axes of symmetry, and the Spider Fold has four axes of symmetry.

Half Fold

1. Colored side up, valley-fold in half, forming a white rectangle. Crease sharply.

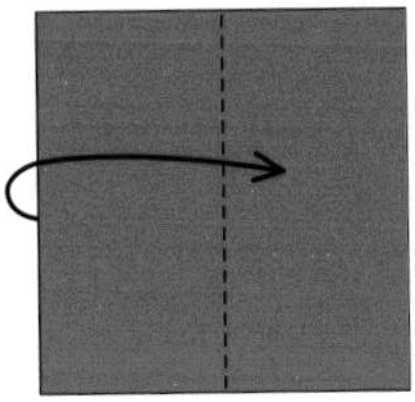

2. Draw or trace, noting where the folded edge is located relative to the design. ✡

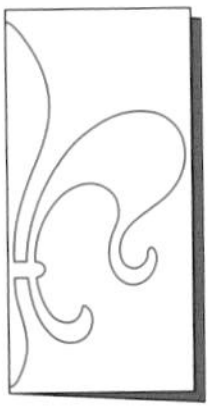

Square Fold

Begin with the Half Fold shown above.

1. Valley-fold in half, forming a white square. Crease sharply.

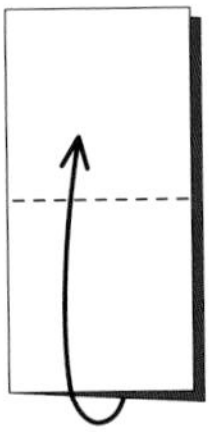

2. Draw or trace, noting where the folded edges are located relative to the design. ✡

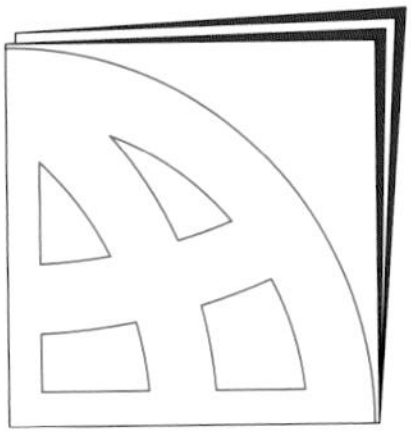

Spider Fold

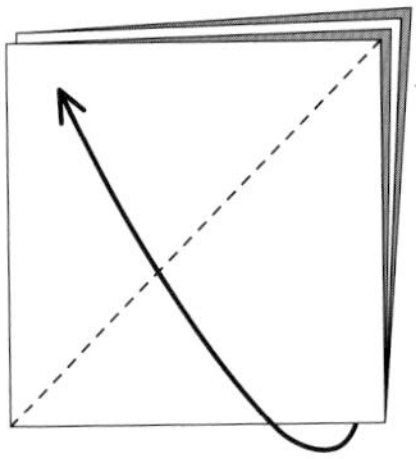

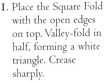

Begin with the Square Fold shown below left.

1. Place the Square Fold with the open edges on top. Valley-fold in half, forming a white triangle. Crease sharply.

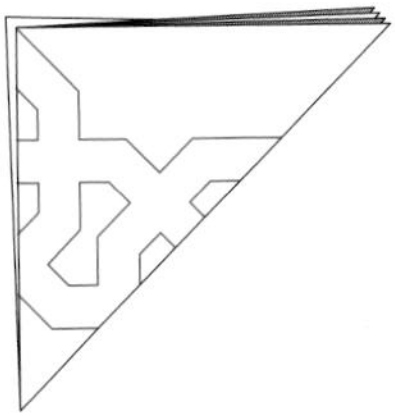

2. Draw or trace, noting where the right-angled side of the triangle is located relative to the design. This corner will be the midpoint of the paper's edges. ✡

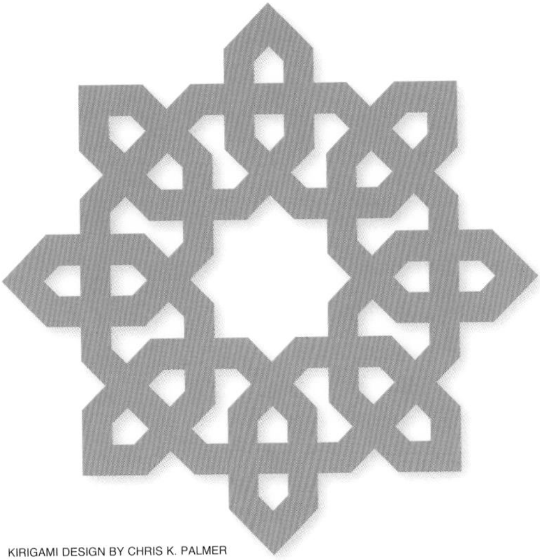

KIRIGAMI DESIGN BY CHRIS K. PALMER

The Snowflake Fold has three axes of symmetry. Six fold lines are 60° from one another. The Angle Set Fold is 60° from the base fold line. Use the template below to mark a square that is 8½ inches, or smaller, folded as shown in step 3.

1. Colored side up, valley-fold in half, forming a white triangle. Crease sharply.

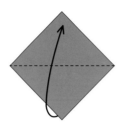

7. Draw or trace the design on either side. ✿

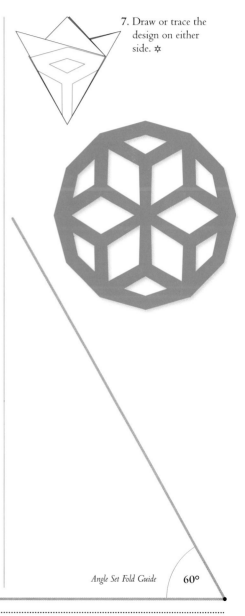

2. Bring the bottom corners together and pinch just the center along the fold line to mark.

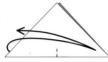

3. Using the angle fold guide drawn on this page, line up the fold line and pinch mark where shown.

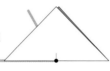

4. Draw a small mark where the upper raw edges of the triangle meet the angle guideline.

5. Valley-fold the left edge of the triangle up on a line connecting the pinch mark from step 2 and the drawn mark from step 4. Crease sharply.

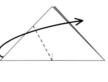

6. Mountain-fold the right corner up so the sloping edge lines up with the right side. Crease sharply.

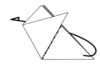

Angle Set Fold Guide   **60°**

The Starburst Fold has five axes of symmetry. Ten fold lines are 36° from one another. The Angle Set Fold is 72° from the base fold line; doubling back these folds bisects the angle to 36°. Use the template below to mark a square that is 8½ inches, or smaller, folded as shown in step 1.

Complete steps 1–2 of the Snowflake Fold on page 17.

1. Using the angle fold guide drawn on the page, line up the fold line and pinch mark where shown.

2. Draw a small mark where the upper raw edges of the triangle meet the angle guideline.

3. Valley-fold the left edge of the triangle up on a line connecting the pinch mark and the drawn mark. Crease sharply.

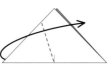

4. Valley-fold the same flap back, in half. Crease sharply.

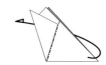

5. Mountain-fold the right corner up so the sloping edge lines up with the right side. Crease sharply.

6. Mountain-fold the same flap back, in half. Crease sharply.

7. Draw or trace the design on either side. ✿

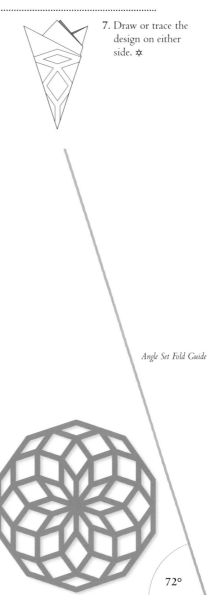

Angle Set Fold Guide

72°

KIRIGAMI DESIGN BY CHRIS K. PALMER

Pleated folds have one axis of symmetry, repeating in regular intervals. This fold is also called a zigzag or concertina fold. Traditional paper dolls and patterned banners such as Mexican paper picado use pleats. Here are a couple of ways to make them, in order of neatness.

ZIGZAG UNTIL THE END OF THE PAPER

Not as neatly folded since the edges tend to "creep" in and out. Useful for large sheets or roll paper to make banners.

1. Colored side up, start with a square, rectangle, or other strip of paper and valley-fold a portion over, keeping the side edges lined up. Crease sharply.

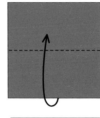

2. Turn over top to bottom.

3. Roll the edge over; make a new fold to line up with the raw edge. Crease sharply.

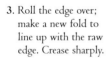

4. Repeat steps **2–3** until the last flap isn't wide enough to meet the other folded edges. Trim this section off.

5. Draw or trace the design on the white or back side. ✻

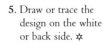

DIVIDE EVENLY, THEN PLEAT

Neater to fold, but with more than three or four divisions, the paper's thickness can make uneven pleats. Useful for quickly dividing any sheet in equal, even-numbered panels.

1. Start with a square, rectangle, or other strip of paper and valley-fold in half. Crease sharply.

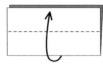

2. Valley-fold in half again, taking care that the layers don't slip out of alignment as you fold. Crease sharply.

3. Repeat step **2** until the desired panel width is achieved.

4. Unfold completely and reverse any folds as necessary so the paper is zigzag-folded.

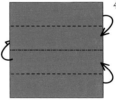

5. Draw or trace the design on the white or back side. ✻

BEKAH GJERDE

EASY PROJECTS
ANYONE CAN CUT

Designed by Chris K. Palmer, this kirigami snowflake is true to form—its hexagonal symmetry is just like that of a real snow crystal. Begin with the Snowflake Fold on page 17.

1. Trace the pattern below onto the Snowflake Fold.

2. Begin cutting the center hexagon with a knife and steel ruler, or begin with a knife and then insert the scissor blade to finish.

3. Hold the paper firmly near the scissor cuts to keep it from slipping. Finish cutting the sides, then the tip, and finally the outer edge.

4. Unfold, and carefully flatten by reversing each fold line. You can place the kirigami between the pages of a heavy book overnight. ✿

Pattern is printed at 100% for a 6-inch square.

The word dendritic means treelike. Dendrites are star-shaped crystals with side branches. Drawn by Pat Kelley, this snowflake resembles a true collection of snow crystals. For more snowflake science, visit papersnowflakes.com. Begin with the Snowflake Fold on page 17.

1. Trace the pattern below onto the Snowflake Fold.

2. Begin cutting the thin center pieces with a knife and steel ruler, or begin with a knife and then insert the scissor blade to finish.

3. Hold the paper firmly near the scissor cuts to keep it from slipping. Finish cutting the sides, then the tip, and finally the outer edge.

4. Unfold, and carefully flatten by reversing each fold line. You can place the kirigami between the pages of a heavy book overnight. ✶

Pattern is printed at 100% for a 6-inch square.

Get ready for Halloween with this easy-to-cut spider web designed by Bekah Gjerde. Spider webs are made of silky threads of viscous fluid that harden when exposed to air. Orb weavers create this type of web design. Naturally, this kirigami paper cut begins with the Spider Fold on page 16.

1. Trace the pattern below onto the Spider Fold.

2. Always begin cutting out the smaller pieces first, but save the corner tip for last! This makes it easier to keep the layers from slipping.

3. Hold the paper firmly near the scissor cuts to keep it from slipping. Finish cutting the sides, then the tip, and finally the outer edge.

4. Unfold, and carefully flatten by reversing each fold line. You can place the kirigami between the pages of a heavy book overnight. ✶

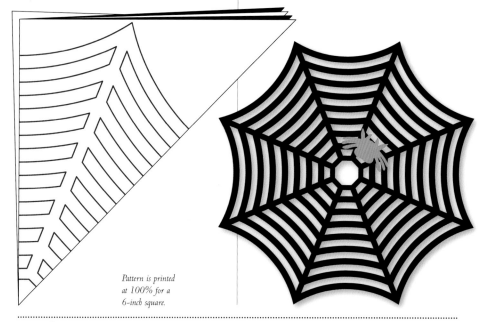

Pattern is printed at 100% for a 6-inch square.

Cindy Higham creates "snowflakes" for all seasons. This colony of creepy critters will complement the Spider Web on the opposite page. Make a hip Halloween treat tote by gluing designs on either side of a shopping bag. Her design was adapted to begin with the Spider Fold on page 16.

1. Trace the pattern below onto the Spider Fold.

2. Always begin cutting out the smaller pieces first, but save the corner tip for last! This makes it easier to keep the layers from slipping.

3. Hold the paper firmly near the scissor cuts to keep it from slipping. Finish cutting the sides, then the tip, and finally the outer edge.

4. Unfold, and carefully flatten by reversing each fold line. You can place the kirigami between the pages of a heavy book overnight. ✷

Pattern is printed at 100% for a 6-inch square.

Frame your favorite photo with this adorable circus-y border. Jeff Cole drew this design and has created several hundred more kirigami paper cuts for his Kirigami *calendars. Begin with the Spider Fold on page 16.*

1. Trace the pattern below onto the Spider Fold.

2. Begin cutting the ear with a knife, or begin with a knife and then insert the scissor blade to finish. Don't cut the whole shape out; just make a flap. Using a ¹/₁₆-inch hole punch for the eye is easier than trying to cut one!

3. Hold the paper firmly near the scissor cuts to keep it from slipping. Finish by cutting the side and corner, and finally the outer edge.

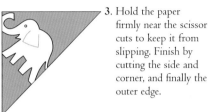

4. Unfold, and carefully flatten by reversing each fold line. Lift each ear flap slightly. If pasting around a picture, don't get glue on the ears. ✿

Pattern is printed at 100% for a 6-inch square.

Silhouetted clip art can be a great resource for making kirigami patterns. The angle of the nose relative to the wings is about 60°—perfect for six-fold symmetry. Begin with the Snowflake Fold on page 17.

1. Trace the pattern below onto the Snowflake Fold.

3. Hold the paper firmly near the scissor cuts to keep it from slipping. Finish cutting the sides, and finally the outer edge.

2. For this piece, cut the tip first, since it's so small.

4. Unfold, and carefully flatten by reversing each fold line. You can place the kirigami between the pages of a heavy book overnight. ✺

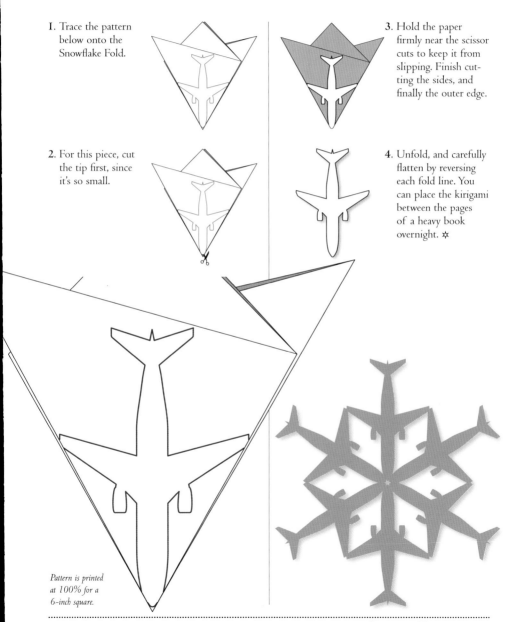

Pattern is printed at 100% for a 6-inch square.

This adaptation of a design by Cindy Higham can decorate a loved one's wrapped gift, or use it as a doily for a romantic dinner. Because it's so simple to cut, try a smaller square to make coasters to match. Begin with the Starburst Fold on page 18.

1. Trace the pattern below onto the Starburst Fold.

3. Hold the paper firmly near the scissor cuts to keep it from slipping. Finish cutting the sides, then the tip, and finally the outer edge.

2. Always begin cutting out the smaller pieces first, but save the corner tip for last! This makes it easier to keep the layers from slipping.

4. Unfold, and carefully flatten by reversing each fold line. You can place the kirigami between the pages of a heavy book overnight. ✳

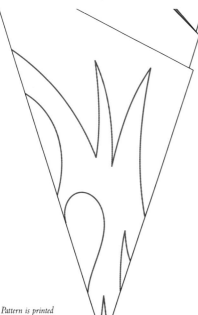

Pattern is printed at 100% for a 6-inch square.

In Roman mythology, Cupid was the god of love. Hearts and arrows form a classic romantic motif in Cindy Higham's ultimate Valentine's Day kirigami. Begin with the Starburst Fold on page 18.

1. Trace the pattern below onto the Starburst Fold.

3. Hold the paper firmly near the scissor cuts to keep it from slipping. Finish cutting the sides, then the tip, and finally the outer edge.

2. Always begin cutting out the smaller pieces first, but save the corner tip for last! This makes it easier to keep the layers from slipping.

4. Unfold, and carefully flatten by reversing each fold line. You can place the kirigami between the pages of a heavy book overnight. ✫

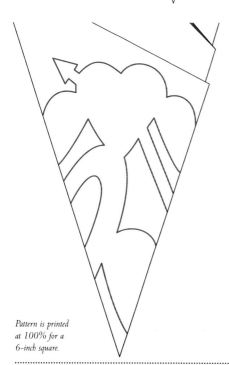

Pattern is printed at 100% for a 6-inch square.

This beautiful design by Bekah Gjerde is a sure sign of spring. Even though the pattern itself is symmetrical, it would be very difficult to cut through more than ten layers of paper. Holding the paper carefully will help you cut evenly on each side. Begin with the Starburst Fold on page 18.

1. Trace the pattern below onto the Starburst Fold.

2. Begin cutting the small square with a knife and steel ruler, or begin with a knife and then insert the scissor blade to finish. Save the small tip for last.

3. Make knife slits in the heart and the enclosed shape below; then insert the scissor blade to accurately cut the curves. Hold the paper firmly near the scissor cuts to keep it from slipping.

4. Unfold, and carefully flatten by reversing each fold line. You can place the kirigami between the pages of a heavy book overnight. ✿

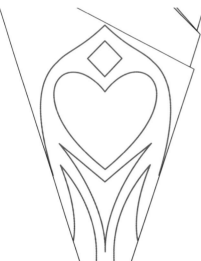

Pattern is printed at 100% for a 6-inch square.

This delicate pattern looks deceptively simple, but it does require a bit of skill with knife and scissors. Cut this kirigami from tissue paper and hang in a window for sunshine even on cloudy days. Begin with the Spider Fold on page 16.

1. Trace the pattern below onto the Spider Fold.

3. Hold the paper firmly near the scissor cuts to keep it from slipping. Cut the larger pieces, then the edges. Save the tip for last.

2. Begin cutting the inside smaller wedges with a knife and steel ruler, or begin with a knife and then insert the scissor blade to finish.

4. Unfold, and carefully flatten by reversing each fold line. You can place the kirigami between the pages of a heavy book overnight. ✣

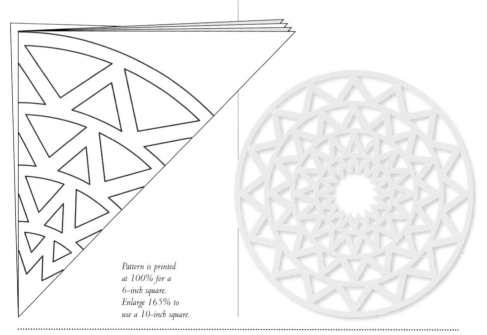

Pattern is printed at 100% for a 6-inch square. Enlarge 165% to use a 10-inch square.

Kathy Monahan created this design inspired by a coworker's Celtic Cross necklace. She combined two of her favorite passions: Celtic art and paper cutting. Begin with the Spider Fold on page 16.

1. Trace the pattern below onto the Spider Fold.

2. Begin cutting the small teardrop with a knife, or begin with a knife and then insert the scissor blade to finish.

3. Hold the paper firmly near the scissor cuts to keep it from slipping. Cut the remaining inside of the piece, then the edges.

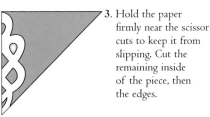

4. Unfold, and carefully flatten by reversing each fold line. You can place the kirigami between the pages of a heavy book overnight. ✽

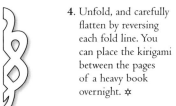

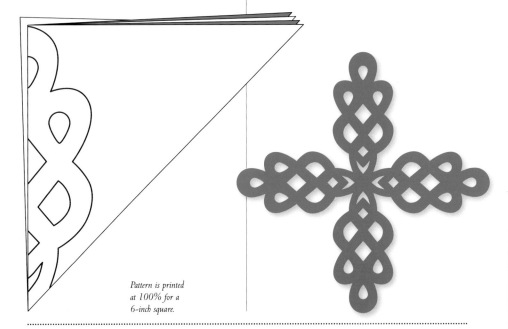

Pattern is printed at 100% for a 6-inch square.

The Celtic Knot has been used as a stylized representation of knots and braids by many cultures, and was often drawn in Christian manuscripts such as the 8th-century Book of Kells. This design is from Jeff Cole's 21st-century Kirigami Calendar. Begin with the Snowflake Fold on page 17.

1. Trace the pattern below onto the Snowflake Fold.

2. Begin cutting the inside curved shapes with a knife, or begin with a knife and then insert the scissor blade to finish.

3. Hold the paper firmly near the scissor cuts to keep it from slipping. Finish cutting the sides, and finally the outer edge.

4. Unfold, and carefully flatten by reversing each fold line. You can place the kirigami between the pages of a heavy book overnight. ✿

Pattern is printed at 100% for a 6-inch square.

Typically made of lace, doilies were often placed under decorative objects, or cut from napkins for cakes or other sweet foods to rest upon. Jeff Cole designed this frilly doily that looks lovely atop a formal dinner plate. Begin with the Snowflake Fold on page 17.

1. Trace the pattern below onto the Snowflake Fold.

2. Begin cutting the center closed shape with a knife, or begin with a knife and then insert the scissor blade to finish.

3. Hold the paper firmly near the scissor cuts to keep it from slipping. Finish cutting the sides, then the tip, and finally the outer edge.

4. Unfold, and carefully flatten by reversing each fold line. You can place the kirigami between the pages of a heavy book overnight. ✫

Pattern is printed at 100% for a 6-inch square.

Inspired by traditional quilt designs, Bekah Gjerde created this kirigami using simple shapes and just a sliver cut from the edges, lending it a slight contrast from the original square base. Begin with the Spider Fold on page 16.

1. Trace the pattern below onto the Spider Fold.

2. Begin cutting the inside shapes with a knife and steel ruler, or begin with a knife and then insert the scissor blade to finish.

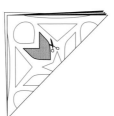

3. Hold the paper firmly near the scissor cuts to keep it from slipping. Cut the slivers from the outside edges *first*, then cut out the remaining pieces. It helps to have the slanted edge intact to hold on to.

4. Unfold, and carefully flatten by reversing each fold line. You can place the kirigami between the pages of a heavy book overnight. ✿

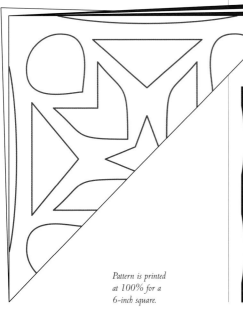

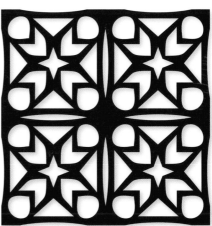

Pattern is printed at 100% for a 6-inch square.

Beatriz Diaz Goodpasture teaches papel picado, and has designed traditional Mexican cut tissue displays for all kinds of events. She has even designed a bridal shower dress cut from paper! Begin with the Pleated Fold on page 19 from any length of tissue paper.

I. Enlarge to the desired size and trace the pattern below onto the Pleated Fold. The raw edges of the paper should be at your left as shown.

raw edges on top and bottom layers

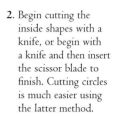

2. Begin cutting the inside shapes with a knife, or begin with a knife and then insert the scissor blade to finish. Cutting circles is much easier using the latter method.

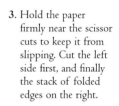

3. Hold the paper firmly near the scissor cuts to keep it from slipping. Cut the left side first, and finally the stack of folded edges on the right.

4. Unfold, and carefully flatten by reversing each fold line. Tape the top edge on the front of a shelf to display. To hang as a garland, measure and trace the design so that about twice the width of the top "frame" can fold over and glue with a long string inside. ✿

To make the banner pictured below, pleat a 36- × 7-inch piece of tissue paper eight times. Enlarge pattern 200%.

Jeff Cole's kirigami meets origami in this clever fold, which is derived from a traditional Waterbomb Base. Use this same technique to make 3-D ornaments from any kirigami design that starts with a Spider, Snowflake, or Starburst pre-fold. Begin with the Spider Fold on page 16.

1. Trace the pattern below onto the Spider Fold.

3. Hold the paper firmly near the scissor cuts to keep it from slipping. Finish cutting the folded edge *first*. Then cut the larger closed shape, tip, and outer edge.

2. Begin cutting the inside shapes with a knife, or begin with a knife and then insert the scissor blade to finish.

4. Unfold, and carefully reverse some fold lines so that there is a Mountain Fold bisecting each tree and a Valley Fold between each ball. Lift up to make the ornament 3-D and glue the insides together one section at a time, aligning the edges carefully. It's only necessary to glue the outer rings together. ✿

Pattern is printed at 100% for a 6-inch square.

Expanding paper with alternating cuts on pleated paper is an old tradition. If you fold a circle and begin cutting a pie-shaped wedge this way it will make a delicate bell-shaped net. Begin with the Spider Fold on page 16.

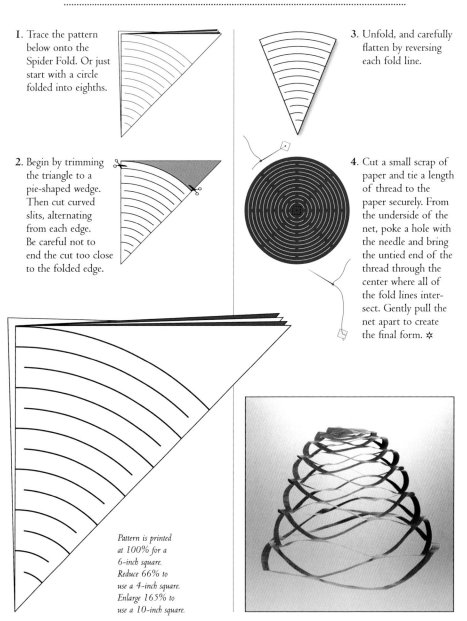

1. Trace the pattern below onto the Spider Fold. Or just start with a circle folded into eighths.

2. Begin by trimming the triangle to a pie-shaped wedge. Then cut curved slits, alternating from each edge. Be careful not to end the cut too close to the folded edge.

3. Unfold, and carefully flatten by reversing each fold line.

4. Cut a small scrap of paper and tie a length of thread to the paper securely. From the underside of the net, poke a hole with the needle and bring the untied end of the thread through the center where all of the fold lines inter-sect. Gently pull the net apart to create the final form. ✫

Pattern is printed at 100% for a 6-inch square. Reduce 66% to use a 4-inch square. Enlarge 165% to use a 10-inch square.

"Net"work a series of Bell Nets to form a chain of ornamental spheres, or make a hanging sculpture with varying sizes and added embellishments. For a chain of orbs, begin with Bell Nets made from 4-inch squares.

BALL GARLAND

1. To make a garland chain of orbs cut the Bell Net pattern from 4-inch squares. For each ball, cut two of the same color.

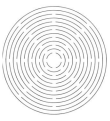

2. Place a tiny drop of glue *in the middle of the first inside cut.* Align a like-colored net atop, making sure the slits match up perfectly. Each set is one orb. Make more!

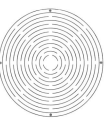

3. Place a more generous drop of glue in the center of one set and align another set atop. Keep gluing sets together in the middle to make as many orbs as you want. Allow the glue to dry.

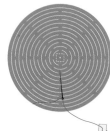

4. Perform step **4** from the Bell Net on the opposite page at each end of your chain. *Gently* stretch apart the orbs to create the final form. You can stretch apart each individual orb by gently pulling it by its neighbors. ✿

FINGER HOLDERS FOR A LARGE ORB

Fold two 1-inch squares of light cardstock. Trace the pattern at left onto them and cut. Unfold and lift up the semicircle ring. Glue one in the center of each side of a 10-inch orb. Stretch! ✿

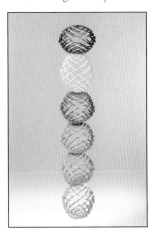

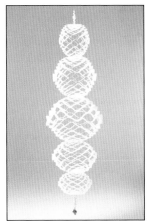

The letters pictured in green, opposite, all share a vertical symmetry. When tracing, however, pay close attention to which side the fold line is on. Begin by cutting seven 6-inch squares into quarters—enough for a complete set from A–Z.

A Trace onto a square, folded in half. Cut and unfold.

J J has a final cut *after* unfolding. Trace onto a square folded in half, marking the secondary cut line shown in black. Cut the lines in blue, unfold, and then trim at the black line.

L L also has a final cut *after* unfolding. Trace onto a square folded in half, marking the secondary cut line shown in black. Cut the lines in blue, unfold, and then trim at the black line.

The fold line is on this side!

M Trace onto a square, folded in half. Cut and unfold.

P P is tricky. Trace onto a square folded in half, marking the secondary cut lines shown in black. Cut the lines in blue just until they intersect the black. Unfold and trim to shape on each side.

The fold line is on this side!

R R is also tricky. Trace onto a square folded in half, marking the secondary cut lines shown in black. Cut the lines in blue just until they intersect the black. Unfold and trim to shape on each side.

The fold line is on this side!

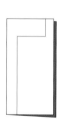

T Trace onto a square, folded in half. Cut and unfold.

U Trace onto a square, folded in half. Cut and unfold.

Enlarge these patterns 300% for 3-inch squares.

This alphabet has been modernized combining the kirigami techniques of Joyce Hwang and the letterforms from the typeface Helvetica. First introduced by Swiss type designer Max Miedinger in 1957, it has become the world's most popular sans-serif font.

V Trace onto a square, folded in half. Cut and unfold.

Y Trace onto a square, folded in half. Cut and unfold.

W Trace onto a square, folded in half. Cut and unfold.

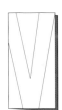

The letters pictured in purple, opposite, all share a horizontal symmetry. When tracing, however, pay close attention to which side the fold line is on. The font Helvetica was adapted for this book because of its near-perfect symmetrical design and universal appeal.

B Trace onto a square, folded in half. Begin cutting the inside shape with a knife, or begin with a knife and then insert the scissor blade to finish. Unfold.

G G is tricky. Trace onto a square folded in half; mark the secondary cut lines shown in black. Cut the lines in blue *first*. Unfold and trim to shape the "G's" upper half.

D Trace onto a square, folded in half. Cut and unfold.

I Trace onto a square, folded in half. Cut and unfold. If your "I" will be the same color as the "E" or "F," simply trim the leftover scrap!

E Trace onto a square, folded in half. Cut and unfold.

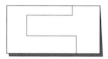

K Trace onto a square, folded in half. Cut and unfold.

F F has a final cut *after* unfolding. Trace onto a square folded in half; mark the secondary cut line shown in black. Cut the lines in blue, unfold, and then trim at the black line.

The fold line is on this side!

Q Trace onto a square folded in half; mark the secondary cut lines shown in black. Cut the lines in blue *first*. Unfold and trim to shape the "Q's" upper half.

Enlarge these patterns 300% for 3-inch squares.

Many other sans-serif fonts can be cut as kirigami, such as Futura, which is based on circular forms. Look for the lines of symmetry and plan your kirigami patterns. Notice how some numbers can easily be made with kirigami, while others can't. Which ones can? Try to cut them!

ABCDEFGHIJ

KLMNOPQR

STUVWXYZ

1234567890

Futura Bold, above, is another font that can be cut as kirigami.

BDEF

GIKQ

The letters pictured in blue share both vertical and horizontal symmetries. When tracing, however, pay close attention to which side the fold line is on. Even though the "S" has perfect symmetry, you might need to practice a few times to make its offset curves look smooth.

C C has two final cuts *after* unfolding. Trace onto a square folded into quarters; mark the secondary cut line shown in black. Cut the lines in blue, unfold, and then trim at the black line, matching up both halves of the "C."

S S is the hardest letter to cut, but by using its symmetry (and a little patience), all of the curves will be correct. Trace onto a square folded into quarters; mark the secondary cut lines shown in black. The dashed line is to help cut the curve on the *other* quadrants. Cut the lines in blue *first*. Unfold and use the template as necessary on other quadrants to trim out the grey areas to shape the final "S."

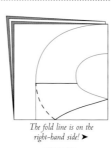

The fold line is on the right-hand side! ►

H Trace onto a square folded into quarters. Cut and unfold.

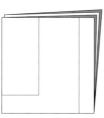

O O is exactly like the "C" except there's no secondary cut! Trace onto a square folded into quarters. Cut and unfold.

X Trace onto a square folded into quarters. Cut and unfold.

Enlarge these patterns 150% for 3-inch squares.

The remaining letters pictured in red share diagonal *symmetry, and in fact are cut using the same pre-fold and pattern. When tracing, however, pay close attention to which side the fold line is on. Now you know your ABCs of kirigami!*

Pre-Fold

1. Colored side up, valley-fold in half, forming a white triangle. Crease sharply.

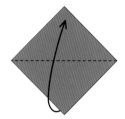

2. Valley-fold in half again from right to left. ✿

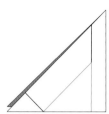

N N has four final cuts *after* unfolding. Trace onto a triangle folded into quarters; mark the secondary cut line shown in black. Cut the lines in blue, unfold, and then trim at the black lines—also trim diagonally across the center fold to match.

Z Repeat the pre-fold steps for "N" followed by the same trace and trimming above. Turn it on its side and now it's a "Z"!

Enlarge the pattern 200% for 3-inch squares.

Ingenious in its simplicity, this easy-to-make twelve-page booklet can contain anything: a pocket phone directory, photo album, or even a little storybook. Draw and color freehand or desktop publish; then print, cut, and fold. Use a letter-size sheet to begin.

1. Set up a layout with the following specs: ½-inch margins on all sides. This leaves an area of 7½ × 10 inches, which divides perfectly into twelve 2½-inch squares.

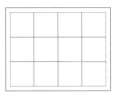

6. Cut through three squares between the top and middle rows, then three squares between the middle and bottom rows. Use a steel ruler and X-Acto for best results.

2. The arrangement and sequence is simple—only the middle row's pages must be rotated 180° as shown.

1	2	3	4
8	7	9	5
9	10	11	12

7. Fold up the Quickiri booklet using the existing folds. Each page folds back-to-back, except for the first and last.

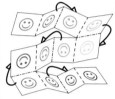

3. Place your pictures, text, or anything else within each box; don't forget to rotate the middle row's images 180°.

8. Use a glue stick to paste the backs of the pages together. You can create a separate cover for the booklet, or lay out the front and back covers and print them on the other side of the sheet before step **4** for a "self-cover." ✷

- Because some inkjet papers have a "good" side, it may be better to print a separate cover that even surrounds the spine. Or use double-sided matte light cardstock.

4. Print and then trim the margins off. Use a steel ruler and X-Acto for best results.

5. Make Mountain and Valley folds as shown. Be precise and crease firmly.

EGOCENTRICITY, 2005, TYVEK, 25" × 25", BY BÉATRICE CORON

Béatrice Coron began her City series in 2001. "I was interested in the flow of thoughts and visions, which give an overview of the dynamism of the city and inner city." Born and raised in Lyon, France, Coron has been living and working in New York since 1984.

CUTTING INTO ANOTHER DIMENSION

Make something really "cool" with this 3-D Snowflake. This traditional design is taught by Liz Peterson to her second-grade class. You'll need six squares of paper, 4 inches or larger, with both sides of the same color. Begin by pre-folding into a triangle, as shown on page 45.

1. Make three cuts from the *single-folded edge* toward the two folded edges, but don't cut all of the way through. Unfold to a square. Repeat until you have six cut squares.

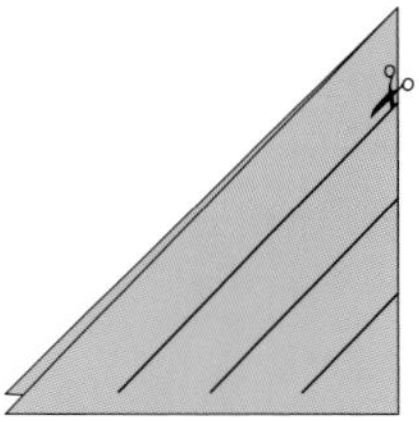

2. Your cut squares should look like this pattern.

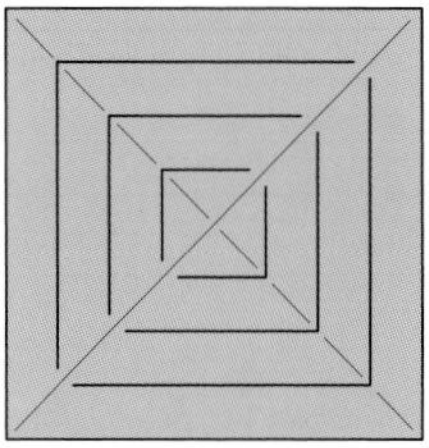

3. Affix the opposite corners of the innermost square with tape, or double-sided tape in between to remain hidden.

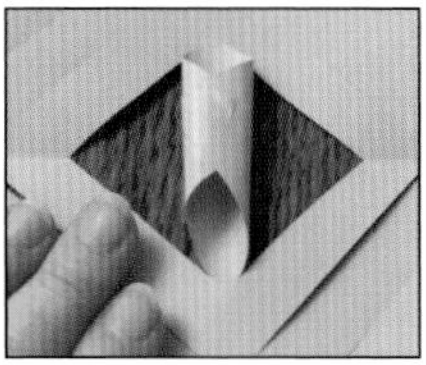

4. *Turn the model over* and join the corners of the next square.

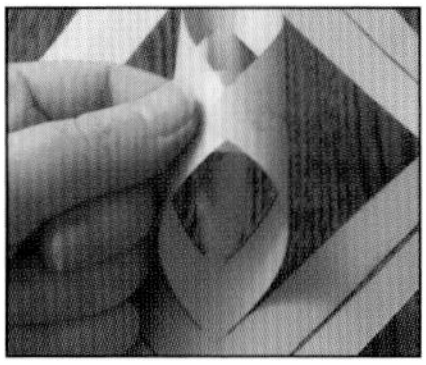

5. Continue to turn the model over before joining the next set of corners until you have a finished module as shown. Repeat for the five remaining cut pieces.

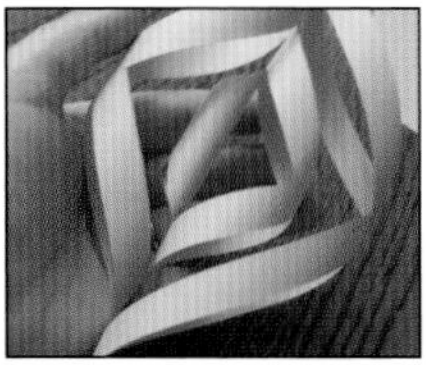

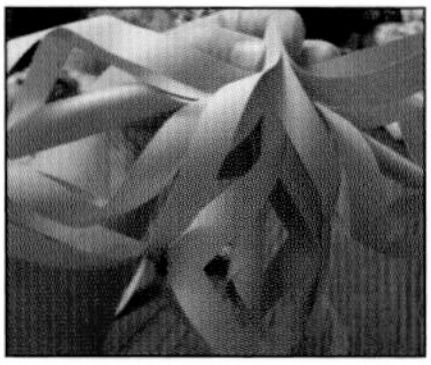

6. Hold three modules together at one end and staple to fasten, or affix double-sided tape for a neater finish. Make another set of three modules.

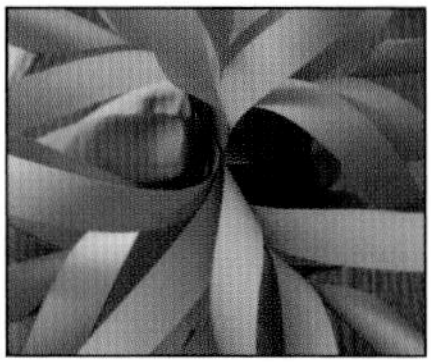

7. Hold both sets of modules together, joining them by overlapping and stapling (or double-sided-taping) to fasten.

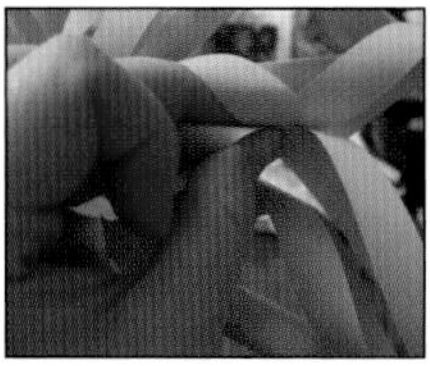

8. Fasten the outermost side of each module to its neighbor. Pierce a hole into one point to hang with a special fiber, yarn, or monofilament thread. ✡

If you use larger paper, or desire more detail, simply cut more than three parallel slits in step 1. Keep the innermost square no less than 1 inch wide to make the first "loop."

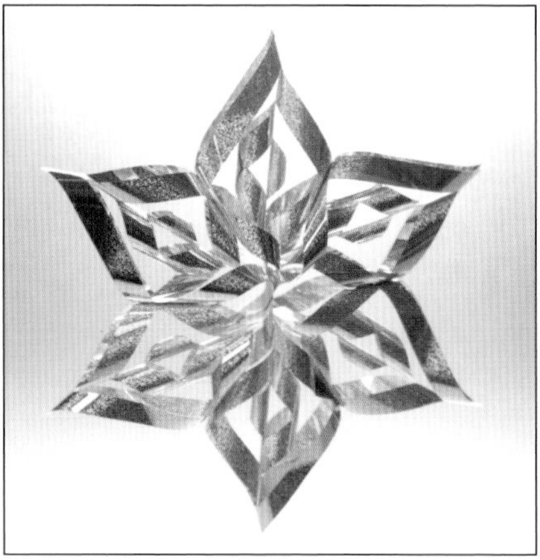

Christiane Bettens makes a 3-D Lucky Clover using kirigami techniques similar to the 3-D Snowflake. This model begins with the traditional Waterbomb Base, familiar to those who fold origami. Use a square of paper, 6 inches or larger, with both sides of the same color.

1. Valley-fold the square in half, parallel to its edges, in both directons. Turn over to the other side.

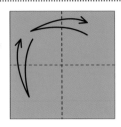

2. Valley-fold the square in half diagonally in both directions. Turn over to the other side.

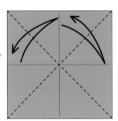

3. While pinching opposite diagonal Mountain Folds, bring your hands down and together, collapsing into four triangular flaps.

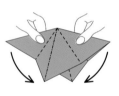

4. Flatten by bringing together two flaps on the left and right.

5. Valley-fold both flaps on the left to the right. Crease firmly.

6. Make four cuts from the *four folded flaps* toward the single folded edge, but don't cut all of the way through. Unfold to a square.

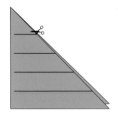

7. Your cut square should look like this pattern.

8. Gather each slit's corner tip together and staple as shown, or affix double-sided tape for a neater finish. Repeat for the three remaining corners. ✿

The Generations technique is used to create hearts within hearts. Use a thin cardstock measuring 8½ × 5½ inches, so that when it's folded in half, it becomes a standard A2 invitation-size card. A2 envelopes are readily available.

1. Score the card at the halfway mark. For help with scoring, see pages 12–13. Carefully fold in half. Crease firmly.

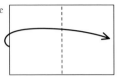

2. Trace the pattern onto the card by using either a stylus or #12 crochet needle to transfer the cut lines from your tracing, or use a pushpin to make a prick at about ⅛-inch intervals. Score Mountain Folds on the outside and Valley Folds on the inside, making sure they are parallel.

3. Cut on cut lines marked with an X-Acto knife. Begin with the innermost cuts first.

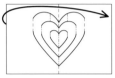

4. *Slowly and carefully* fold the card in half—as you fold, crease the heart shapes on their respective score lines. Refer to the photo below as you fold. Once all of the creases are made, flatten the card to set the folds.

An X-ray view at left shows the complexity of all of the flaps folding flat, ready to pop into 3-D when opened. Glue on a backing card if you wish to hide the large cutout when folded. ✻

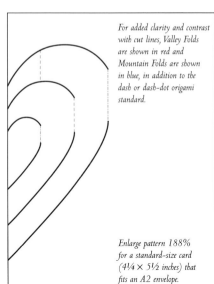

For added clarity and contrast with cut lines, Valley Folds are shown in red and Mountain Folds are shown in blue, in addition to the dash or dash-dot origami standard.

Enlarge pattern 188% for a standard-size card (4¼ × 5½ inches) that fits an A2 envelope.

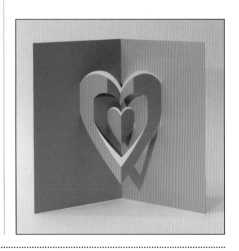

Paul Jackson is one of the world's greatest paper engineers. He designed this charming pop-up as an example of the Wings technique. The secret is simple: two shapes must fold up equidistant from the center fold. You can apply this technique to many other related but different shapes.

1. Trace the pattern onto a 10½- × 5¼-inch thin cardstock. Score the card at the center, heart, and arrow folds. Cut on the cut lines with an X-Acto knife, using a steel ruler for the straight lines.

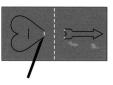

2. Score a same-size backing card at the center mark.

3. Glue the backing card on the back of the cutout, taking care not to get any adhesive onto the heart or arrow. *Immediately* fold cards in half, keeping them aligned at their edges. Allow the glue to dry while folded.

4. Lift the heart and arrow and insert the arrow into the slit made in the heart. Make sure the card opens and closes easily; if necessary widen the slit to allow the arrow to move freely. ✷

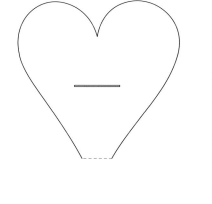

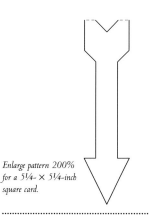

Enlarge pattern 200% for a 5¼- × 5¼-inch square card.

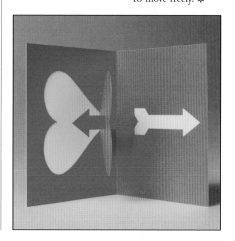

This impressive sculpture can be cut from metalliclike cardstocks such as Stardream (see page 106). Hang near a window to cast beautiful plays of light and shadow as it gently rotates. Once you understand the technique, try it with other shapes, and make a mobile (see page 58).

1. Trace the pattern onto a 9- × 9-inch piece of cardstock.

Score the card on the fold lines shown. Unless it's a really thick stock, you only need to score on one side for both Mountain and Valley folds.

Cut on the cut lines with an X-Acto knife and steel ruler. Begin in the center, working your way toward the outside edges.

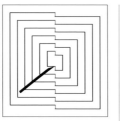

2. Starting at the outside edges, twist the first square at a 90° angle to the second square. Continue by twisting the third, fifth, and center pieces to achieve the final form.

3. Use a pushpin or needle to poke a small hole through the edge of the outermost square, centered with the vertical fold lines. Hang with a monofilament thread. ✿

Enlarge pattern 400% for a 9-inch-square model.

💡 *If making a mobile, you may want to create smaller versions. Enlarge the pattern at left 200% for a 4½-inch model, a perfect size, especially when combined with Concentric Circles.*

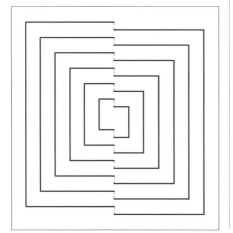

DESIGN BY PAUL JACKSON

The same technique used for cutting Concentric Squares can be modified to include perpendicular axes of symmetry—in this case creating a stunning display simulating orbiting planets or electrons. Combine this model with Concentric Squares and make a mobile (see page 58).

1. Trace the pattern onto a 10- × 10-inch piece of cardstock.

   Score the card on the fold lines shown. Unless it's a really thick stock, you only need to score on one side for both Mountain and Valley folds.

   Cut on the cut lines with an X-Acto knife. When cutting curves it helps to move the paper as you cut. Begin in the center, working your way toward the outside edges.

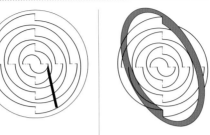

2. Starting at the outside edges, twist the first circle at a 90° angle to the second circle. Continue by twisting the third circle 90° *perpendicular* to the second. Repeat with the remaining pieces to achieve the final form.

3. Use a pushpin or needle to poke a small hole through the edge of the outermost circle, centered with the vertical fold line directly beneath. Hang with a mono-filament thread. ✿

Enlarge pattern 400% for a 9-inch-circle model.

- ☼ *If making a mobile, you may want to create smaller versions. Enlarge the pattern at left 200% for a 4½-inch model, a perfect size, especially when combined with Concentric Squares. For a tree ornament, enlarge 150% for a 3⅜-inch "ball."*

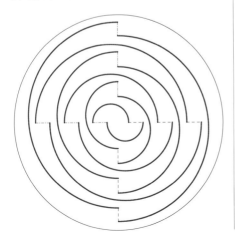

Designed by Peter Visser, this clever desk calendar is simple to make; the challenge is what to adorn the sides with. You could print important phone numbers, photos, work-related ephemera... or let your kids draw on it before you put it together!

1. Photocopy or scan the patterns (page 84) at 150% for a 5-inch-tall model. It just fits letter size as shown, but you may want to print onto legal size (grey area) if your printer doesn't print to the edge. Alternatively, you could scan or copy at 148% with virtually no noticeable difference.

   Print onto a medium-weight cardstock. You could also photocopy or print the pieces onto differently colored cardstock.

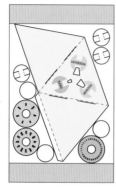

2. Score the long Valley Fold lines on the tetrahedron, and the short lines on each wheel axle. Cut on the cut lines with an X-Acto knife and steel ruler. Begin with the date, day, and month windows, then the adjacent thin slits. Next cut the straight lines on the tabs for each axle and then the tetrahedron's outline.

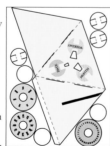

3. Cut out all of the other parts.

Enlarge patterns, page 84, 150% for a 5-inch-tall model (base is 5¾ inches on each side). Enlarge 200% for a 6⅝-inch-tall model (base is 7⅞ inches on each side).

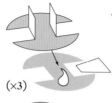
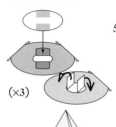

(×3)

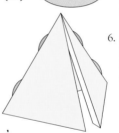

(×3)

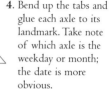

4. Bend up the tabs and glue each axle to its landmark. Take note of which axle is the weekday or month; the date is more obvious.

5. Insert the date, weekday, and month wheels onto the axles. Fold down the tabs and apply glue sparingly to each tab. Affix a cap to each.

6. Assemble tetrahedron by folding on scored lines and gluing tab to edge. ✳

💡 *Use desktop publishing to arrange photos, phone lists, etc. Lay out your custom art using the sized scan as a guide onscreen. Print onto cardstock, or have a copy shop laserprint or enlarge it for you.*

TETRAHEDRAL MAP PROJECTION BY CARLOS FURUTI

Mark Hiner's clever trillium diamond-shaped card demonstrates one of the many tricks paper engineers use to create surprise up-pops. When removed from its envelope, it will "spring up" into shape. You'll need heavyweight cardstock for this model, and a small, strong rubber band.

1. Trace the up-pop pattern (page 85) on the *back side* of heavyweight card stock. Score all of the Valley Folds onto the same side; score the three small Mountain Folds on the *reverse* side. Cut out the pieces using an X-Acto knife and steel ruler, but *do not cut on the orange lines yet!*

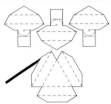

2. Cut out a 10½- × 5¼-inch card; score down the middle and use a pushpin to mark the glue areas.

3. Mountain-fold the tabs on the three bottom pieces and glue securely. When dry, carefully trim along the orange lines, leaving a tiny triangular hole and a slit.

4. Valley-fold the bottom pieces along their scores. Glue into place at the marked area of the card. Repeat with the remaining two bottom pieces.

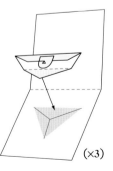

(×3)

Enlarge pattern, page 85, 200% for a 5¼-inch-square card.

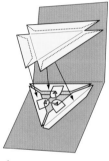

💡 *Square envelopes are available in some specialty paper stores, or see page 106. Alternatively, make a bottom card to fit any sturdy envelope you choose.*

5. Slide a small, strong rubber band between the slits in each tab to hold the bottom pieces upright as shown. Test a few sizes to get just the right amount of tension: not too tight so that the sides buckle; not too loose so it won't quickly pop up when opened. Test a few times before step 6.

6. Glue the tabs from the top piece securely onto the flat edges of the bottom pieces, hiding the rubber-band mechanism. Insert it into an envelope and spring on your intended. ✿

Many kirigami designs, and other papercraft models, make great mobiles. The design pictured is the Classic Snowflake on page 22. You can glue two pieces of the same design back-to-back for added stiffness, or cut one out whole using the pattern below.

BEAD AND WIRE MOBILES

Mobile structures can be made in a variety of ways—from two sticks that cross each other to a complex set of masts that balance. Many types of material can also be used. To purchase materials for the bead and wire mobile pictured, see page 106.

1. Cut out as many snowflakes, or other designs, as you want in your mobile. Poke a small hole near the top, and tie a length of monofilament thread to each.

2. Bead and wire mobiles are made using ⅛-inch-long bits of flexible tubing that slip over a monofilament thread and a steel mast. This allows endless adjustments to easily change a model.

Enlarge 150% for a 3⅜-inch snowflake.

3. Plan your mobile by drawing an idea first. This idea is only an example. Then cut masts with wire cutters and the beads with scissors. Insert thread through the bead and carefully insert the mast's end into the bead, all held snugly by friction.

4. Trial and error is the best way to find an arrangement that looks nice, balances, and allows the models to spin without hitting one another. The advantage of this system is you can adjust the beads, positions, and lengths of thread in minute amounts until it's just perfect! ✷

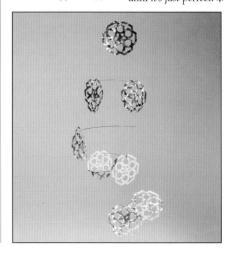

Eric Gjerde makes an origami tessellation inspired by M. C. Escher. Many patterns of repeated elements make beautiful cutaways. Place near a window and watch the play of light and shadow create an endless exhibit. Begin with a letter-size, lightweight cardstock.

1. Enlarge and trace the pattern. Score the fold lines. When using a lightweight cardstock, you can score all folds on one side for this design.

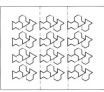

2. Cut on the marked lines using an X-Acto knife and steel ruler.

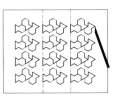

3. Crease the long vertical folds first; then flip out each fish as you like; you don't have to follow the folds as marked. ✫

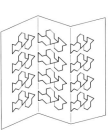

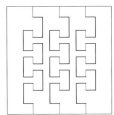

Paper engineer Paul Jackson has taught this simple technique to great effect.

Create your own unique designs by beginning with simple shapes!

Try other patterns by using the templates shown here.

Enlarge the pattern below left 375%, rotate 90° clockwise, and center on letter-size cardstock.

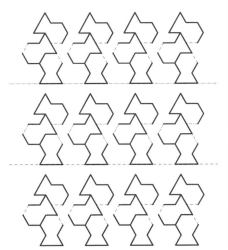

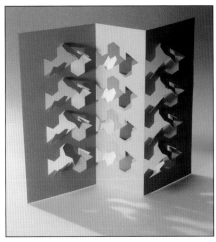

David Hathaway created these clever cube lattices. When carefully folded and glued, they are perfect for mobiles, ornaments, or just desktop curios. This model is easy to assemble, but patience is key to making it perfect!

1. Accurately score all of the Valley Folds. Begin cutting the inside tabs with an X-Acto knife and steel ruler; then cut out the rest of the model.

2. Pre-fold all of the scored lines.

3. Using glue *sparingly*, "roll" all of the inside beams and affix the tab onto the inside of the cube's faces. There are 12 beams.

4. Assemble the cube faces by gluing the remaining outside tabs to the sides of the tabless squares to form the final shape. ✼

GLUE TAB HERE

GLUE TAB HERE

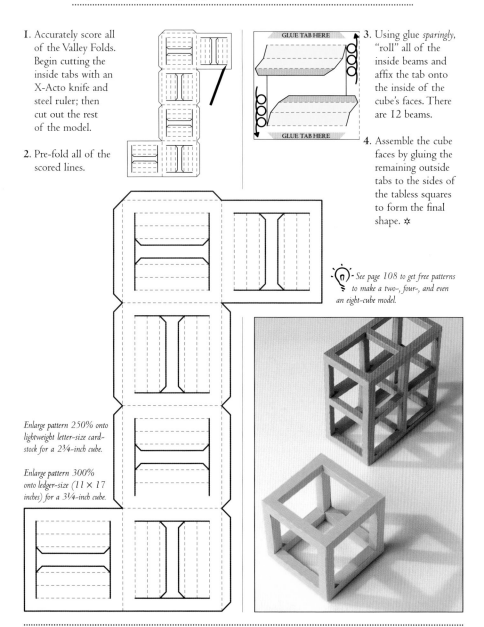

- *See page 108 to get free patterns to make a two-, four-, and even an eight-cube model.*

Enlarge pattern 250% onto lightweight letter-size cardstock for a 2¾-inch cube.

Enlarge pattern 300% onto ledger-size (11 × 17 inches) for a 3¼-inch cube.

Keiko Nakazawa began studying an art form created by Masahiro Chatani called origamic architecture. Nakazawa and Chatani are prolific authors and co-authors. When kirigami meets origami, incredible forms can take shape.

1. Trace both patterns (pages 86–87) onto lightweight card-stocks of different colors (one pattern for each color). Score *exactly* in the middle as shown, then cut the shapes precisely with an X-Acto knife.

2. Mountain-fold the two lower-left portions to the back of card "B" as shown by the dotted lines.

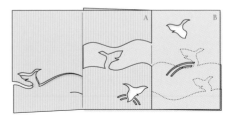

3. Slip card "A" in between the upper-left portions as shown. Check top and side alignment, then glue in place.

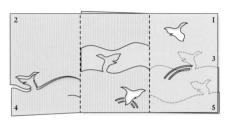

4. Using the numbered flaps and the photos as a guide, fold each portion to the center, in order. Then tuck the top edge of flap 5 into the slot in flap 4 to lock. ✿

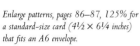
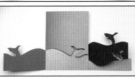

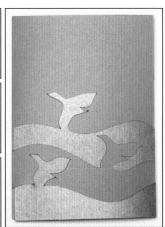

Enlarge patterns, pages 86–87, 125% for a standard-size card (4½ × 6¼ inches) that fits an A6 envelope.

Chris K. Palmer has combined geometry and art to create remarkable tessellations, silk pleatings, geometric containers, and many other origami-based models. This family of polar zonohedra are assembled by cutting and weaving only two versions of a single "S" curve. Math can be beautiful!

1. *Organization of the parts* (pages 88–89) is key to weaving this model correctly the first time. Cut out the eight parts of each "S" curve. Keep them in separate piles and oriented as shown. *It's very easy to get them turned around or flipped over accidentally, and you won't realize it until the ends are ready to be locked together.*

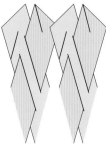

(×8)

2. Make eight sets of "X" shapes by weaving part A through part B, going under and over the center of the strip. Double-check that the ends all match the areas circled in the diagram.

3. Connect the sets to one another as shown. You should have one long, curled strip of sixteen "S" curves. Double-check again that the ends all match the areas circled in the diagram above.

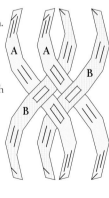

4. Bring the edges together and weave the centers to complete a cylinder. Now you are ready to finish weaving.

Enlarge the patterns, pages 88–89, 130% for a 4- × 6-inch model. Enlarge 200% for a 6- × 9-inch version.

5. After you've woven all of the strips together, the ends should converge as shown.

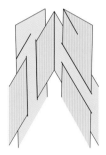

6. The last step is to lock adjacent sets, slipping the tabs together so the "ends" are on the *inside* of the model. Tweezers—as well as a bit of perseverance—will be helpful getting the last sets together! ✻

By varying the shape of the "S" curve, an infinite range of models can be made. In a darkened room, hold the model in front of a flashlight to cast dynamic, mandala-like diffraction-pattern shadows on the wall as shown on page 48.

George W. Hart is an artist and educator whose geometric sculptures are simple, complex, and beautiful—all at the same time. This model is one of a series of Slide-togethers he created using regular polygons that assemble into unique geometric constructions.

1. Trace or print the pattern on five differently colored lightweight cardstocks. Cut out the 20 triangles with an X-Acto knife and steel ruler. It's easier to cut the slits first; then cut apart the four triangles of each color.

2. Begin by sliding one color into another. Pick an order so that your model will not have two triangles of the same color touch. The order here is red, orange, yellow, green, and blue.

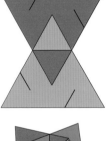

3. Complete a "star" of all five colors, in order, as shown. Make another set.

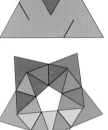

(×2)

4. Slide five triangles into one of the "stars" you made in step 3, creating a "belt"; the ball-like shape will begin to form. Add one more belt, using up all of your loose triangles. Remember the color order you set!

5. Finish the model by orienting the remaining "star" so the colors are in their correct positions.* If you didn't assemble the pieces correctly the first time, they're easy to slide apart and rearrange until you get it right! ✶

No two triangles of the same color will ever touch each other.

💡 *As you may have guessed, this is as much a puzzle as it is a modular kirigami sculpture—and that's just how Hart wants it! An Internet link to free patterns for more Slide-together puzzles, information on modular kirigami, and his incredible geometry-based art, can be found on page 108.*

Enlarge the pattern 250% for a 6-inch-diameter model. Trace or print onto five differently colored lightweight cardstocks for a total of 20 triangles with slits.

(×5)

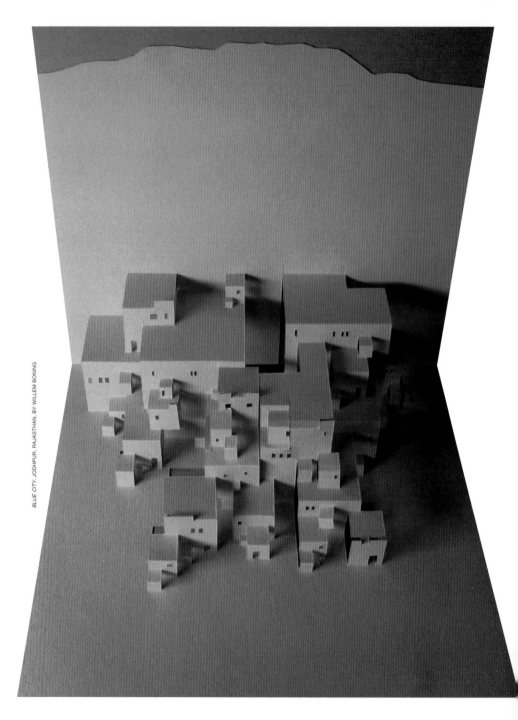

BLUE CITY, JODHPUR, RAJASTHAN, BY WILLEM BONING

How to Be
a Paper
Architect

Introduction

Origamic architecture, or "OA," is where origami meets kirigami meets pop-ups. OA combines the precise folding of origami, the detailed cutting of kirigami, and the ingenious paper engineering of pop-ups. Origamic architecture is a growing art form, and was pioneered by architect and civil engineer Masahiro Chatani in 1981.

> *"After trying for some time to design original greeting cards, I finally designed some unique pop-up cards by folding and cutting paper. When you open one of these folded, post-card sized constructions, there is a wondrous movement and a structure arises which is so interesting and fascinating that it captures your attention."*
>
> —Masahiro Chatani,
> *Pop-Up Origami Architecture,* 1984

0°, 90°, 180°, and 360°

OA models are usually cut and folded from one sheet of paper. Folded flat, they can be mailed in standard envelopes, or stored conveniently. When you open an OA greeting card, magic happens as it pops up into a three-dimensional structure. Most structures are known as 90° models, and are displayed standing up. Some models are meant to be displayed opened flat; these are 180° cards. There are a few where you open the card 360°, so that the back and front come together. Masahiro Chatani and Keiko Nakazawa have designed many of these amazing types, like the *3-D Die* pictured below. A few, at 0°, are like

REPETITION 2004, BY INGRID SILIAKUS

overlapping collages, such as the Plover Greeting Card (pictured on page 61). However, they are still just as ingenious!

Most OA artists—such as Ingrid Siliakus from The Netherlands, Joyce Aysta and Chris Hankinson from the United States, and Tatyana Stolyarova from Russia—credit their interest in the art to one of Chatani or Nakazawa's books.

Another published artist, Ramin Razani, is a designer from Italy who has merged his love of OA with the modern lighting products he creates. *Luar Limbo* lamps by Fernando Sierra of Colombia are cut and folded from just one long strip of paper (pictured on page 109).

Although mass-produced, laser-cut OA cards are available to purchase, this section will teach you how to make a variety of architectural and sculptural works of art yourself!

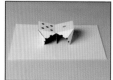

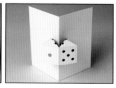
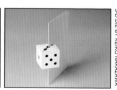

3-D DIE BY KEIKO NAKAZAWA

Enlarge, Transfer, and Cut the Pattern

Use a photocopier or scanner to enlarge to size. The percentages are given both on the model's page as well as the corresponding pattern page. In addition to the methods outlined on the following project pages, here are some additional tips.

Mount the pattern onto the cardstock with masking tape, or other easily removable tape.

Trace the pattern onto the card with a pushpin, marking the endpoints of straight lines to be folded and cut; for curved lines prick at about ⅛-inch intervals.

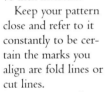

Keep your pattern close and refer to it constantly to be certain the marks you align are fold lines or cut lines.

Score with a #12 crochet needle for thin cardstock, or cut lightly with an X-Acto for thick cardstock, then cut your model.

Flex, Fold, and Flatten

After all the cuts have been made, begin by creasing the center folds. Flex the card while using your fingers to pop out the areas that are mountain-folded, and push in the areas that are valley-folded.

Slowly and carefully fold the card in half—as you fold, be sure that each element is popping out, or pushing in, from the center fold. Refer to the diagram and model photo constantly. Once all of the creases are made, flatten the card to set the folds.

Make a Backing Card, if Desired

Most of the models look great when just light is allowed to show through, and thus don't need further embellishment. However, you may wish to have a contrasting color as a front and back of the card, or to give it extra support to mail.

Cut *two separate pieces*, one sized for the front and one for the back. While flattened, sparingly glue each side to the areas that do not move. Two pieces are necessary so the center fold will still move freely. There are additional ways to display your models. See the Artist's Resources section on pages 107–108 for Web sites with more examples. ✶

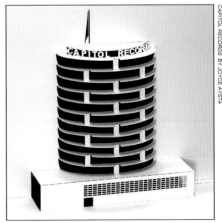

The Generations technique is used in this simple example that demonstrates how to "generate" more pop-ups by adding successive cuts and creases. The number of pop-ups doubles with each generation.

1. Trace the pattern (page 90) onto the card by using either a stylus or #12 crochet needle to transfer the cut and fold lines from your tracing, or use a pushpin to make a prick at the beginning and end of each line.

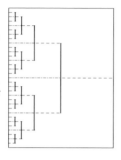

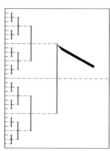

3. Cut on the cut lines with an X-Acto knife and a steel ruler.

2. If you choose a thick cardstock, score Mountain Folds on the *front* and Valley Folds on the *back*, by lightly cutting with an X-Acto knife and steel ruler only halfway through, making sure everything is parallel.

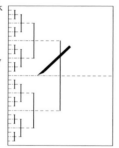

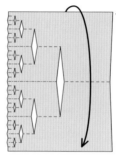

4. *Slowly and carefully fold the card in half—as you fold, crease the steps on their respective score lines. Refer to the photo below as you fold. Once all of the creases are made, flatten the card to set the folds.* ✻

For a thin cardstock, use the stylus and a steel ruler to score Mountain Folds on the *back* and Valley Folds on the *front*.

Enlarge pattern, page 90, 160% for letter-size cardstock.

René Bui is an artist and art educator. He has a Web site devoted to paper crafts, as well as other art forms. The Visitor's Section encourages people to contribute their work to share ideas and foster the teaching of art in as many ways as possible. See page 107 for more information.

1. Trace the pattern (page 91) onto the card by using either a stylus or #12 crochet needle to transfer the cut and fold lines from your tracing, or use a pushpin to make a prick at the beginning and end of each line; for the curved lines use a pushpin to make a prick at about ⅛-inch intervals.

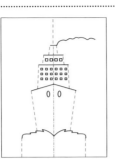

2. If you choose a thick cardstock, score Mountain Folds on the *front* and Valley Folds on the *back*, by lightly cutting with an X-Acto knife and steel ruler only halfway through.

   For a thin cardstock, use the stylus and a steel ruler to score Mountain Folds on the *back* and Valley Folds on the *front*.

3. Cut on the straight cut lines with an X-Acto knife and a steel ruler. Begin with the windows, then the anchor hawseholes. Next cut the slit coming from the smokestack and continue with the remaining lines.

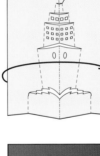

4. *Slowly and carefully* fold the card in half—as you fold, pop the barge and waves from the back on their respective score lines. Refer to the photo below as you fold. Once all of the creases are made, flatten the card to set the folds. ✿

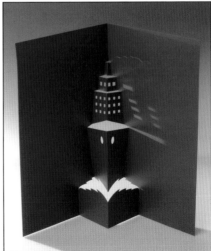

Enlarge pattern, page 91, 160% for letter-size cardstock.

This model can benefit from cardstocks with a softer texture. Designer Laura Badalucco suggests that a backing sheet not be used so that light can filter through the different levels.

1. Trace the pattern (page 92) onto the card by using either a stylus or #12 crochet needle to transfer the cut and fold lines from your tracing, or use a pushpin to make a prick at the beginning and end of each line; for the curved lines use a pushpin to make a prick at about ⅛-inch intervals.

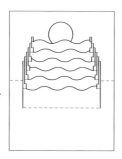

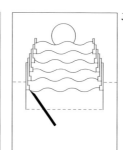

3. Cut the *curved* lines first, then cut the straight lines from the inside out with an X-Acto knife and a steel ruler. Be careful not to tear the strips connecting the waves.

4. *Slowly and carefully* fold the card in half—beginning with the central fold. Place your hand behind the waves to coax them out; if the scores are set, the card will form its shape easily. Once all of the creases are made, flatten the card to set the folds. ✿

2. If you choose a thick cardstock, score Mountain Folds on the *front* and Valley Folds on the *back*, by lightly cutting with an X-Acto knife and steel ruler only halfway through.

For a thin cardstock, use the stylus and a steel ruler to score Mountain Folds on the *back* and Valley Folds on the *front*.

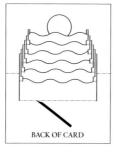

BACK OF CARD

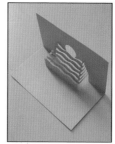

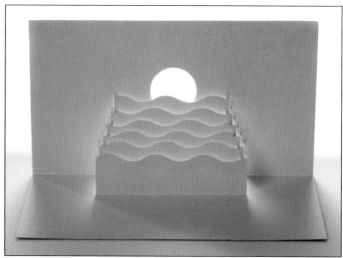

Enlarge pattern, page 92, 160% for letter-size cardstock.

Masahiro Chatani designed this clever creature. He has written many books; unfortunately, most are out of print. However, if you search used book resellers on the Internet, a number of great titles are available to purchase.

1. Trace the pattern (page 93) onto the card by using either a stylus or #12 crochet needle to transfer the cut and fold lines from your tracing, or use a pushpin to make a prick at the beginning and end of each line; for the curved lines use a pushpin to make a prick at about ⅛-inch intervals.

2. If you choose a thick cardstock, score Mountain Folds on the *front* and Valley Folds on the *back*, by lightly cutting with an X-Acto knife and steel ruler only halfway through.

   For a thin cardstock, use the stylus and a steel ruler to score Mountain Folds on the *back* and Valley Folds on the *front*.

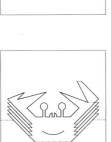

BACK OF CARD

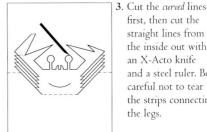

3. Cut the *curved* lines first, then cut the straight lines from the inside out with an X-Acto knife and a steel ruler. Be careful not to tear the strips connecting the legs.

4. *Slowly and carefully* fold the card in half—beginning with the central fold. Place your hand behind the crab to coax him out; if the scores are set, the card will form its shape easily. Once all of the creases are made, flatten the card to set the folds. ✿

Enlarge pattern, page 93, 160% for letter-size cardstock.

Designed by Masahiro Chatani, this example of his origamic architecture demonstrates several pop-up techniques from previous models in this book. The difference between most pop-up cards and origamic architecture is that origamic cards are cut from a single sheet of paper.

1. Trace the pattern (page 94) onto the card by using either a stylus or #12 crochet needle to transfer the cut and fold lines from your tracing, or use a pushpin to make a prick at the beginning and end of each line.

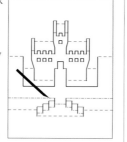

3. Cut the windows and crenelations first, then cut the straight lines from the inside out with an X-Acto knife and a steel ruler.

4. *Slowly and carefully* fold the card in half— beginning with the central fold. Place your hand behind the steps in front first to coax them out a bit; then work on the larger walls. If the scores are set, the card will begin to form its shape. Once all of the creases are made, flatten the card to set the folds. ✿

2. If you choose a thick cardstock, score Mountain Folds on the *front* and Valley Folds on the *back*, by lightly cutting with an X-Acto knife and steel ruler only halfway through.

For a thin cardstock, use the stylus and a steel ruler to score Mountain Folds on the *back* and Valley Folds on the *front*.

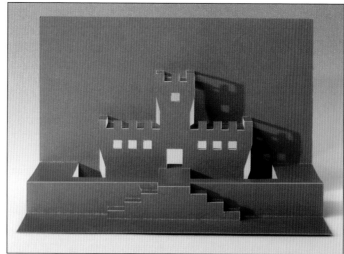

Enlarge pattern, page 94, 160% for letter-size cardstock.

MODERN TOWER

This great, easy-to-make, 180° pop-up card was designed by Magdalena Jonikas. Many creators of origamic architecture—who have advanced degrees in mathematics, the sciences, civil engineering, and architecture—design pop-ups as a hobby. Geometry remains the crux of all paper engineering.

1. Trace the pattern (page 95) onto the pieces. Label each piece "A" and "B" respectively. Make sure they are oriented as shown.

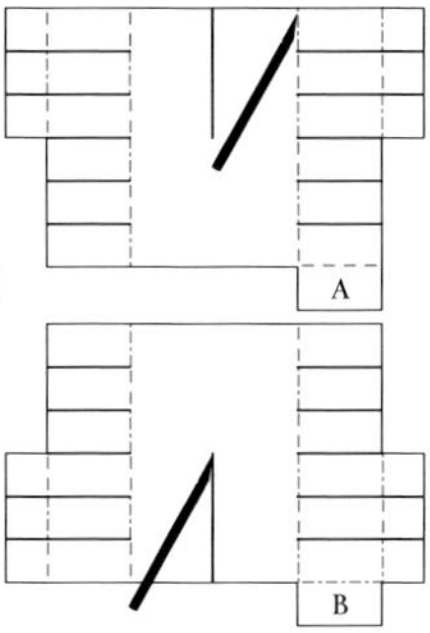

2. If you choose a thick cardstock, score by lightly cutting with an X-Acto knife; for a thin cardstock, use a stylus.

3. Cut on the cut lines with an X-Acto knife. Keep all lines straight and parallel.

4. Flip over part "B" and insert into part "A" so the bottom tabs are in the positions shown.

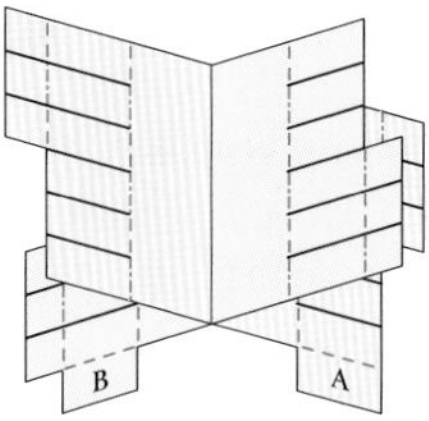

   Make all folds along their scores, referring to the photo if necessary. The smaller, square tabs will be glued to the *inside* of the longer tab it folds closest to.

5. Begin gluing the tabs (shown in grey) to the longer flaps that make up the building's sides. Repeat for the other three sides. Valley-fold up the tabs labeled "A" and "B."

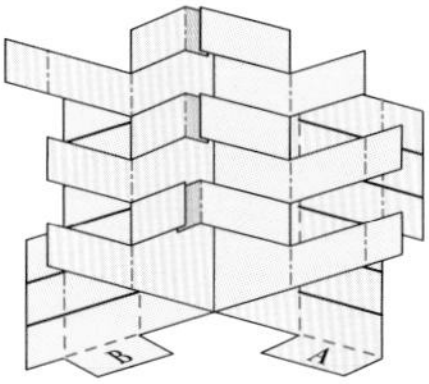

6. Enlarge the card base 200% and mark the corresponding "A" and "B" areas. Score the card base along its center fold. Glue the "A" and "B" flaps to the card base. Hold to set, and allow the glue to dry before opening and closing the Modern Tower. ✫

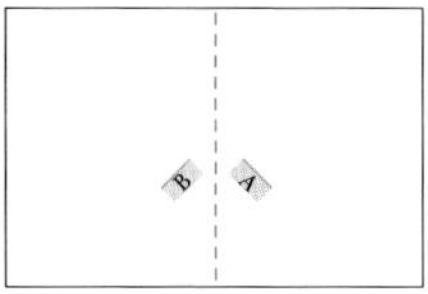

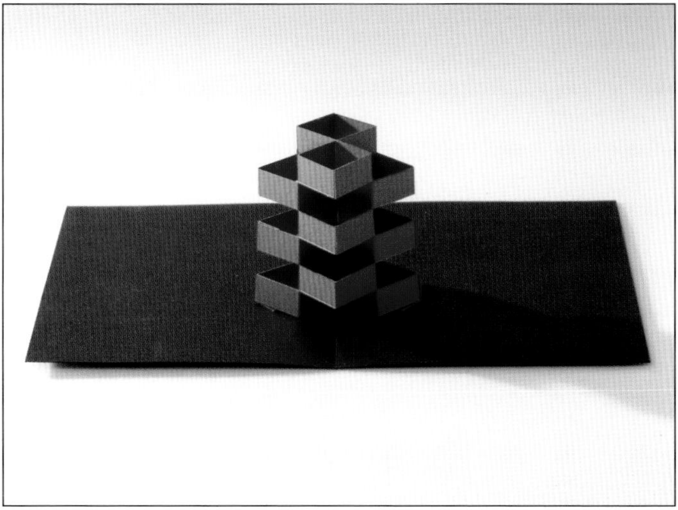

Pattern, page 95, is printed at 100%. Enlarge card base 200% for a standard-size card (4¼ × 5½ inches) that fits an A2 envelope.

René Bui contributed his rendition of this famous landmark. In 1930, Shreve, Lamb & Harmon Associates created the world's tallest building—a record held for over forty-two years. The economy was poor at the time, and the unlet space led it to be nicknamed "the Empty State Building."

1. Trace the pattern (page 96) onto the card by using either a stylus or #12 crochet needle to transfer the cut and fold lines from your tracing, or use a pushpin to make a prick at the beginning and end of each line.

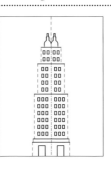

2. If you choose a thick cardstock, score Mountain Folds on the *front* and Valley Folds on the *back*, by lightly cutting with an X-Acto knife and steel ruler only halfway through.

For a thin cardstock, use the stylus and a steel ruler to score Mountain Folds on the *back* and Valley Folds on the *front*.

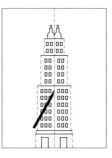

3. Cut the windows first. It's easier if you position your steel ruler along the edges of a row of windows and make the same-side cuts in a row. Then cut the top, side slits, and doors.

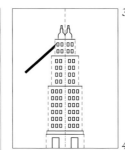

4. *Slowly and carefully* fold the card in half—beginning with the central fold. Place your fingers behind the building sides to pop them out. If the scores are set, the card will begin to form its shape. Once all of the creases are made, flatten the card to set the folds. ✶

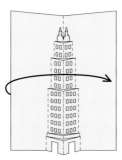

Enlarge pattern, page 96, 160% for letter-size cardstock.

Chris Hankinson was inspired by Masahiro Chatani and started designing his own pop-up cards in 1987. After producing many custom projects for corporate clients, he quickly gained an international reputation as a leader in three-dimensional paper design.

1. Trace the pattern (page 97) onto the card by using either a stylus or #12 crochet needle to transfer the cut and fold lines from your tracing, or use a pushpin to make a prick at the beginning and end of each line; for the curved lines use a pushpin to make a prick at about ⅛-inch intervals.

2. If you choose a thick cardstock, score Mountain Folds on the *front* and Valley Folds on the *back*, by lightly cutting with an X-Acto knife and steel ruler only halfway through.

   For a thin cardstock, use the stylus and a steel ruler to score Mountain Folds on the *back* and Valley Folds on the *front*.

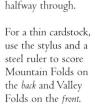

If you have a ¹⁄₁₆-inch punch, cut out the small circle after you begin to pop out the folds.

3. Begin with her crown, her eye,* and the small slits. Then cut the base windows, and finally the remaining lines, always working from the center outward.

4. *Slowly and carefully* fold the card in half—beginning with the central fold. Place your fingers behind the base, then her body and slowly coax the folds into place. The close parallel folds in her lower part are difficult! Take your time and use tweezers if necessary. Once all of the creases are made, flatten the card to set the folds. ✲

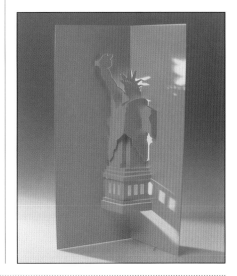

Enlarge pattern, page 97, 160% for letter-size cardstock.

Willem Boning has created models from his travels throughout Europe and Asia. The beginning of this chapter (page 64) features one of a collection of pieces made from sketches and memory during a two-month tour across India.

1. Trace the pattern (page 98) onto the card by using either a stylus or #12 crochet needle to transfer the cut and fold lines from your tracing, or use a pushpin to make a prick at the beginning and end of each line.

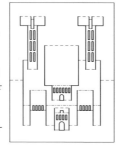

2. If you choose a thick cardstock, score Mountain Folds on the *front* and Valley Folds on the *back*, by lightly cutting with an X-Acto knife and steel ruler only halfway through.

   For a thin cardstock, use the stylus and a steel ruler to score Mountain Folds on the *back* and Valley Folds on the *front*.

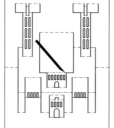

3. Cut the windows and arched doors first, then cut the straight lines. It's easier if you position your steel ruler along the edges of a row of windows and make the same-side cuts in a row.

4. *Slowly and carefully* fold the card in half—beginning with the central fold. Place one hand behind the roofs; use your other hand to pull out the pillars and walls. Once all of the creases are made, flatten the card to set the folds. ✶

Enlarge pattern, page 98, 160% for letter-size cardstock.

Jagoda Djuran designed this south view of the Erechtheion, located on the Akropolis in Athens. This is one of the most unusual and enigmatic buildings ever constructed by the ancient Greeks. The Maiden Porch has attracted the attention of artists and scholars alike. Djuran's original schematic for this design is shown on page 82.

1. Trace the pattern (page 99) onto the card by using either a stylus or #12 crochet needle to transfer the cut and fold lines from your tracing, or use a pushpin to make a prick at the beginning and end of each line; for the curved lines use a pushpin to make a prick at about ⅛-inch intervals.

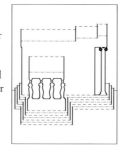

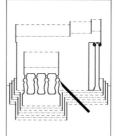

2. If you choose a thick cardstock, score Mountain Folds on the *front* and Valley Folds on the *back*, by lightly cutting with an X-Acto knife and steel ruler only halfway through.

For a thin cardstock, use the stylus and a steel ruler to score Mountain Folds on the *back* and Valley Folds on the *front*.

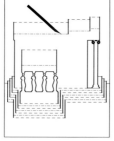

3. Cut the maidens and the column first, then cut the straight lines. Optionally, you can cut the Ionic detail on the column.

4. *Slowly and carefully* fold the card in half—beginning with the upper-half's easier folds. The steps are tricky, and need to be coaxed out carefully to avoid bending the fragile cutouts of the maidens. If the scores are set well, the steps will begin to form their shape. Take your time and use tweezers if necessary. ✱

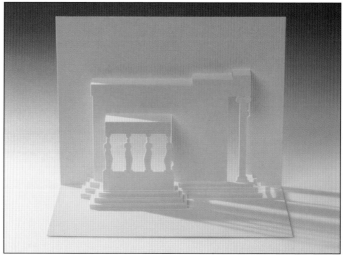

Enlarge pattern, page 99, 160% for letter-size cardstock.

This creation by Tatyana Stolyarova is a 180° pop-up card that uses a technique called Sliceforms, which interlock several pieces together with slits. Similar shapes decrease proportionally in size to give the illusion of roundness.

1. Trace the patterns* (pages 100–101) onto *thin* cardstock by using either a stylus or #12 crochet needle to transfer the cut and fold lines from your tracing, or use a pushpin to make a prick at the beginning and end of each line; for the curved lines use a pushpin to make a prick at about ⅛-inch intervals.

2. Cut out the pieces beginning with the seed pods of Center Pieces A and B. Next cut out the interiors of each piece, then the exteriors. Lastly, cut out the thin slits, being careful not to rip the shapes. Use a steel ruler to help with the long slits of the Center Pieces.

Note that only the Outer Pieces are the same; all other pieces differ slightly by their slits' positions.

The patterns, pages 100–101, are printed at 100% for a standard-size card (4¼ × 5½ inches) that fits an A2 envelope.

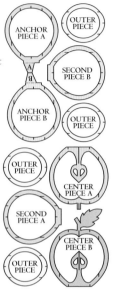

*Colored shapes above are only to help distinguish the different pieces; you should cut your pieces from one color of thin cardstock.

3. Insert Center Piece A onto Center Piece B. Flex the paper slightly to lock at the stem.

4. Hook Anchor Piece B onto Center Piece B, making sure the tab "B" is offset to the *left* when viewed from the outside of the Apple. Repeat for Anchor Piece A, hooking onto Center Piece A, making sure the tab "A" is offset to the *right* when viewed from that side of the Apple.

Stolyarova has created simplified versions of dynamic 180° pop-ups that originally were designed by painstakingly linking together hidden threads glued with tiny pieces of Japanese rice paper. Chatani and Nakazawa's "sliced" models use this more complicated method.

5. Hook Second Piece A onto the "A" side and Second Piece B onto the "B" side. Flex the paper slightly as you weave in between the sections to lock the slits in place.

6. Finally, hook the four outer pieces onto each side, flexing the paper slightly to lock the slits in place.

Enlarge pattern 200% for a standard-size card (4¼ × 5½ inches) that fits an A2 envelope.

7. Enlarge the pattern below 200%, or simply use the reference points to mark the slots where tabs "A" and "B" will insert. Score the card down the middle, cut the slots, and fold in half to set. Open the card and carefully insert tab "A" into the left-hand slot, and tab "B" into the right-hand slot. Test the model to be sure it closes and opens smoothly, and doesn't peek out of the card's edges when closed. Tape or glue the tabs in place. Choose a backing cardstock to hide the tabs. ✿

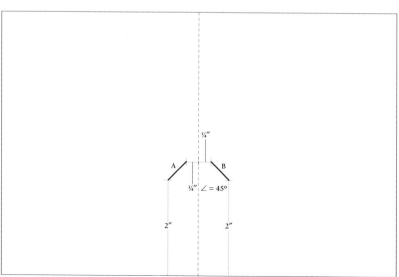

Tatyana Stolyarova is a graphic designer and photographer from Russia who's relatively new to origami architecture and pop-up design compared to mentors like Chatani and Nakazawa. However, she has created her own very intricate and articulated models in the last few years.

1. Trace the pattern (page 102) onto the card by using either a stylus or #12 crochet needle to transfer the cut and fold lines from your tracing, or use a pushpin to make a prick at the beginning and end of each line; for the curved lines use a pushpin to make a prick at about ⅛-inch intervals.

2. If you choose a thick cardstock, score Mountain Folds on the *front* and Valley Folds on the *back*, by lightly cutting with an X-Acto knife and steel ruler only halfway through.

   For a thin cardstock, use the stylus and a steel ruler to score Mountain Folds on the *back* and Valley Folds on the *front*.

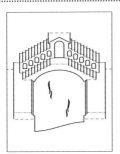

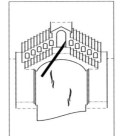

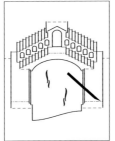

3. Cut the arched windows and waves first, then cut the straight lines from the inside out. Take extra care of the thin, long strips near the water's edge.

4. *Slowly and carefully* fold the card in half—beginning with the central fold and bridge. If the scores are set well, the steps will begin to form their shape. Take your time and use tweezers if necessary. Save the front edge near the water for last. This is a delicate model, so patience is key to success! ✫

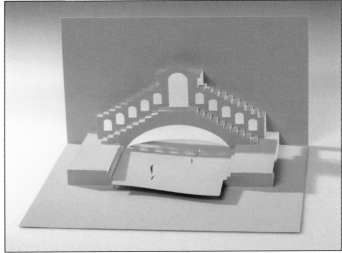

Enlarge pattern, page 102, 160% for letter-size cardstock.

Ramin Razani is one of the world's leading designers in many disciplines—architecture and lighting are specialties. His famous polypropylene Zzzooolights are charming, but his origamic architecture is graphically simple and abstract. He has made other stylish lamps based on his kirigami paper designs.

1. Trace the pattern (page 103) onto the card by using either a stylus or #12 crochet needle to transfer the cut and fold lines from your tracing, or use a pushpin to make a prick at the beginning and end of each line; for the curved lines use a pushpin to make a prick at about ⅛-inch intervals.

2. If you choose a thick cardstock, score Mountain Folds on the *front* and Valley Folds on the *back*, by lightly cutting with an X-Acto knife and steel ruler only halfway through.

   For a thin cardstock, use the stylus and a steel ruler to score Mountain Folds on the *back* and Valley Folds on the *front*.

3. Cut the curved lines from the inside out. Rotate the paper as you cut for a smoother curved line.

4. Bring up each ring on the pre-scored folds, in sequence, beginning with the center. Each previously "folded" ring will then flip around 360° as each new ring is creased. It's helpful to keep flexing the central fold to coax the ring's movements. Repeat with the remaining rings until you have completed creasing all of the rings.

The photos below demonstrate the rings' movements as the card closes. ✳

Steps 1–2

Step 3

Enlarge pattern, page 103, 160% for a 4¼- × 8½-inch card.

30. Jjtt '85

Jaiдgew

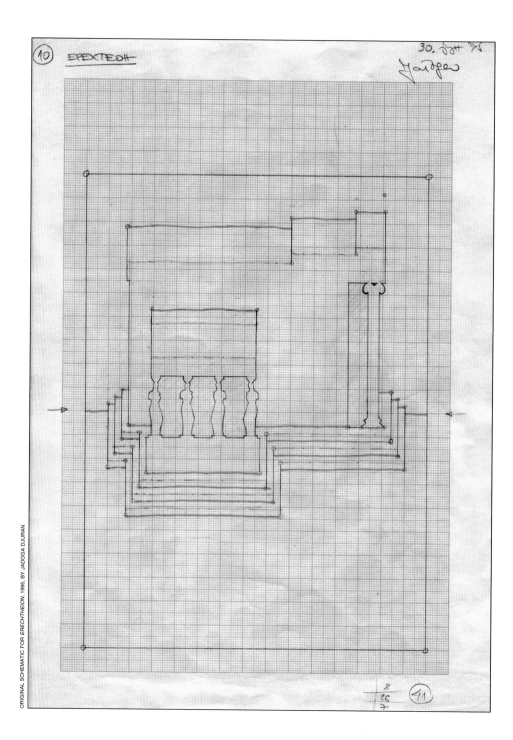

$$\frac{8}{\frac{26}{7}}$$

㊶

PATTERNS

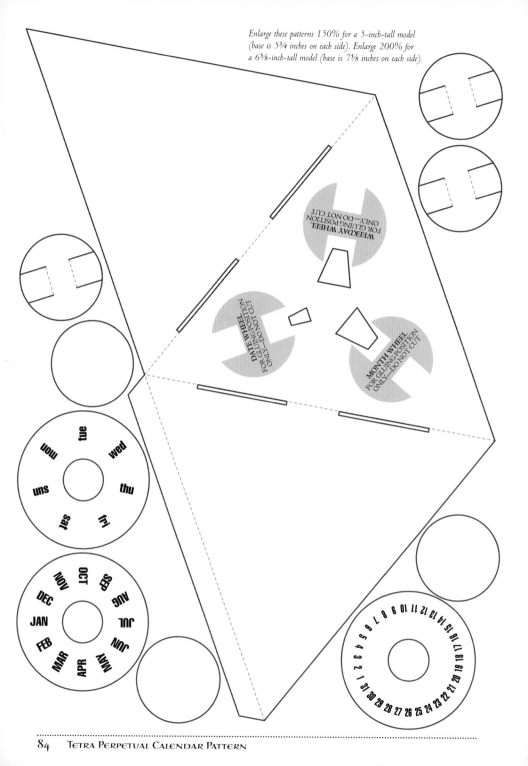

Enlarge these patterns 150% for a 5-inch-tall model
(base is 5¾ inches on each side). Enlarge 200% for
a 6⅝-inch-tall model (base is 7⅝ inches on each side).

WEEKDAY WHEEL
FOR GLUING POSITION
ONLY—DO NOT CUT

DATE WHEEL
FOR GLUING POSITION
ONLY—DO NOT CUT

MONTH WHEEL
FOR GLUING POSITION
ONLY—DO NOT CUT

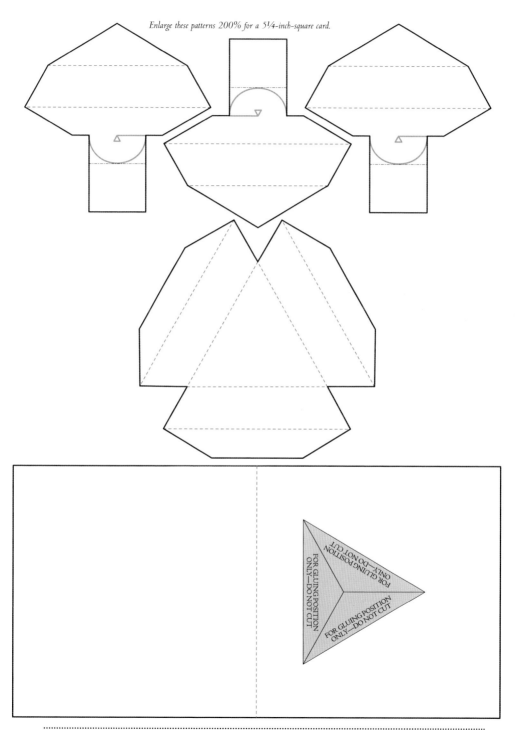

Enlarge these patterns 200% for a 5¼-inch-square card.

FOR GLUING POSITION
ONLY—DO NOT CUT

FOR GLUING POSITION
ONLY—DO NOT CUT

FOR GLUING POSITION
ONLY—DO NOT CUT

Enlarge these patterns 125% for a standard-size card (4½ × 6¼ inches) that fits an A6 envelope.

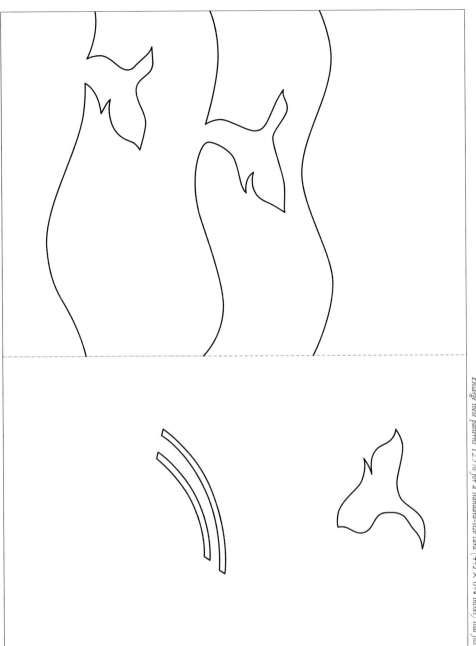

Enlarge these patterns 125% for a standard-size card (4½ × 6¼ inches) that fits an A6 envelope.

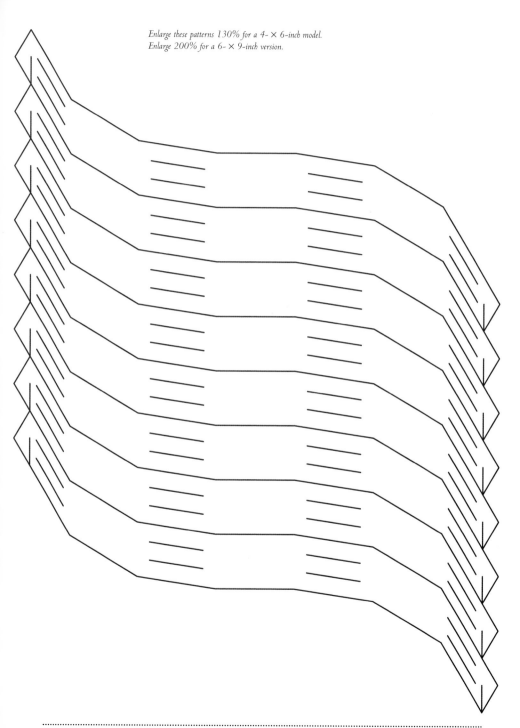

Enlarge these patterns 130% for a 4- × 6-inch model.
Enlarge 200% for a 6- × 9-inch version.

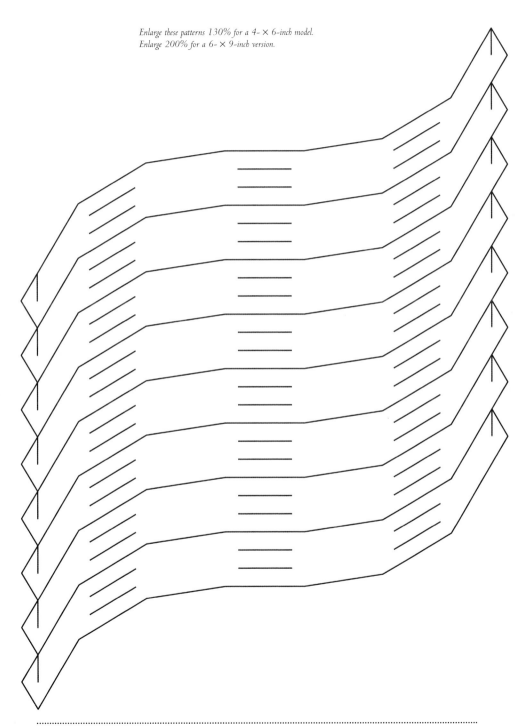

Enlarge these patterns 130% for a 4- × 6-inch model.
Enlarge 200% for a 6- × 9-inch version.

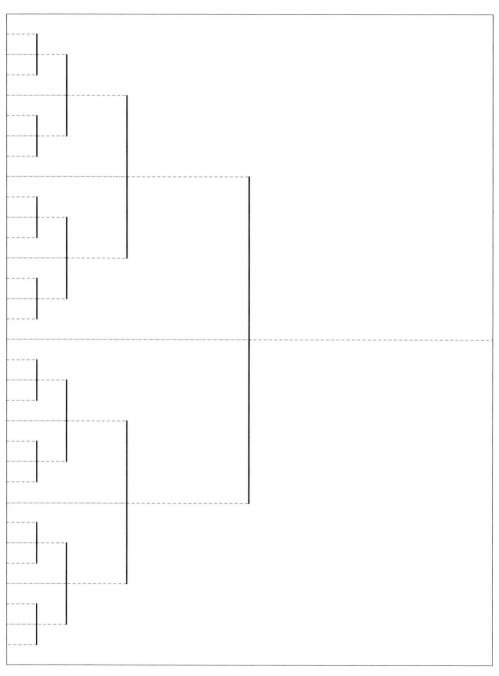

*Enlarge this pattern 160%
for letter-size cardstock.*

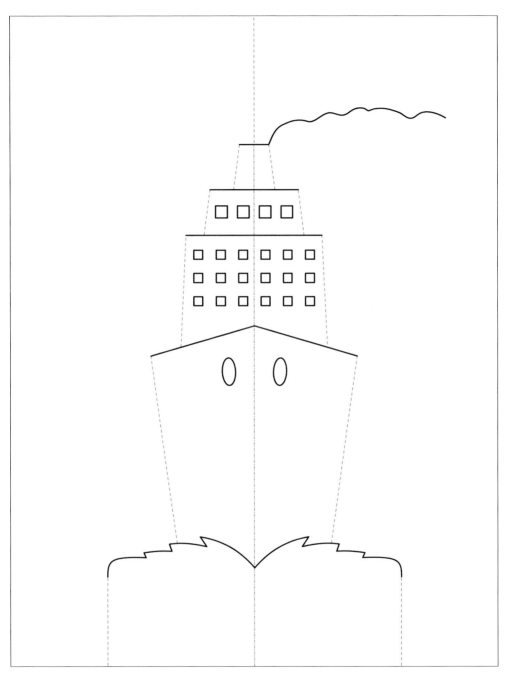

*Enlarge this pattern 160%
for letter-size cardstock.*

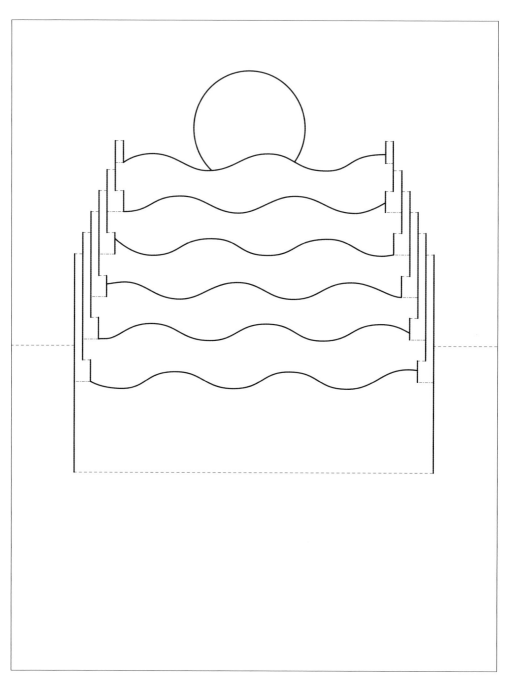

Enlarge this pattern 160%
for letter-size cardstock.

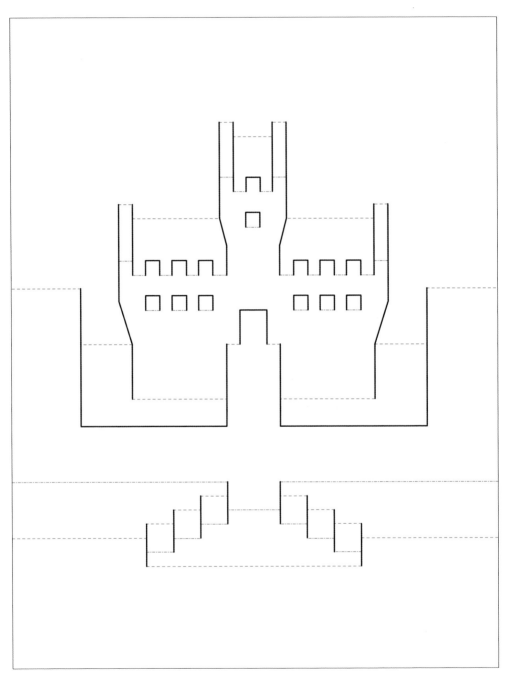

Enlarge this pattern 160%
for letter-size cardstock.

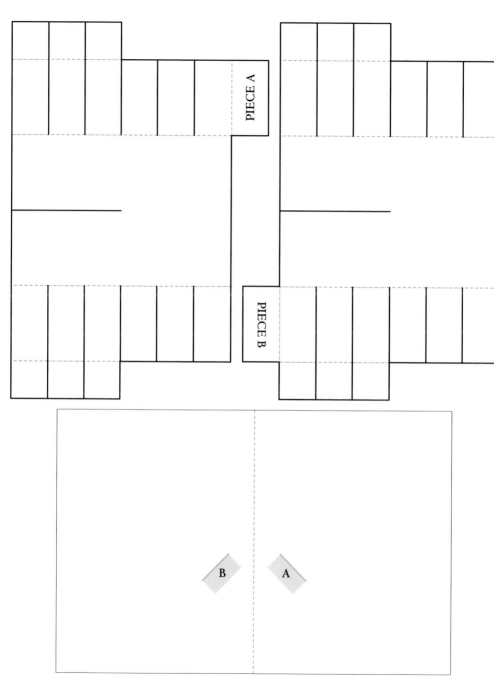

PIECE A

PIECE B

B

A

*Tower pattern is printed at 100%. Enlarge card base 200% for
a standard-size card (4¼ × 5½ inches) that fits an A2 envelope.*

*Enlarge this pattern 160%
for letter-size cardstock.*

*Enlarge this pattern 160%
for letter-size cardstock.*

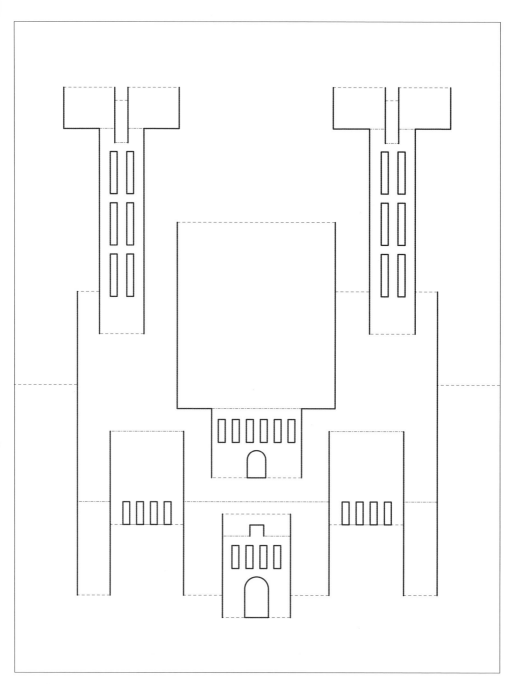

*Enlarge this pattern 160%
for letter-size cardstock.*

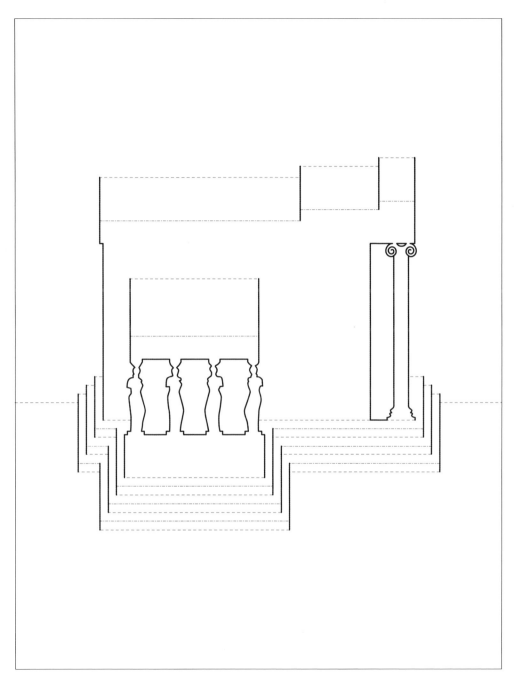

*Enlarge this pattern 160%
for letter-size cardstock.*

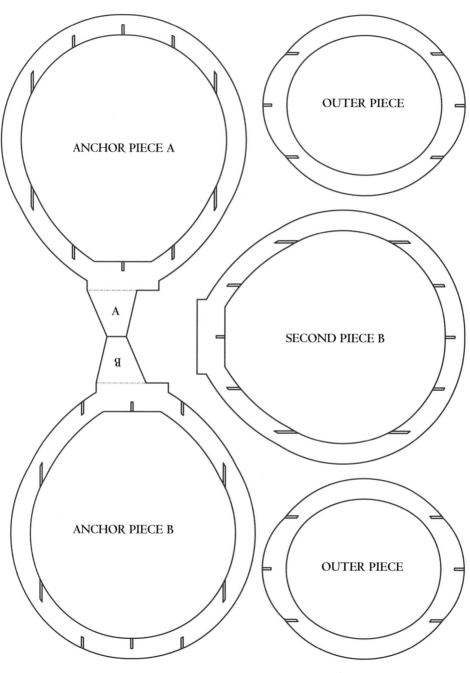

ANCHOR PIECE A

OUTER PIECE

A

B

SECOND PIECE B

ANCHOR PIECE B

OUTER PIECE

*Green Apple patterns are printed
at 100% for a standard-size card.*

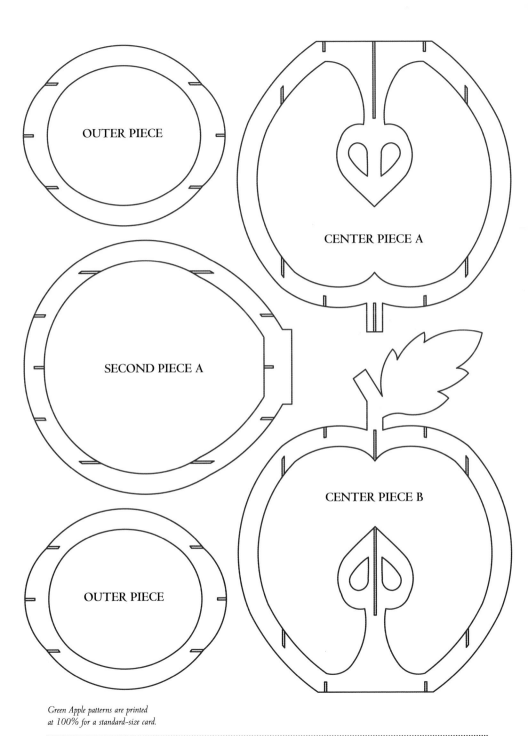

OUTER PIECE

CENTER PIECE A

SECOND PIECE A

CENTER PIECE B

OUTER PIECE

*Green Apple patterns are printed
at 100% for a standard-size card.*

*Enlarge this pattern 160%
for letter-size cardstock.*

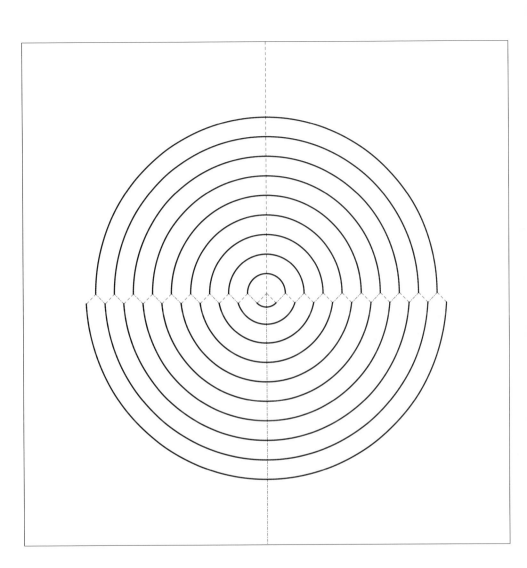

Enlarge this pattern 160%
for a 4¼- × 8½-inch card.

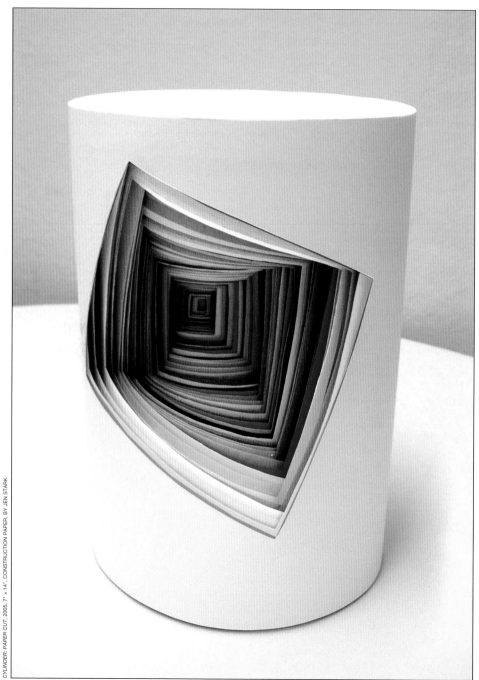

ARTIST'S
RESOURCES

POLAR LIGHT, 2006, BY CHRIS K. PALMER

models in this book is called Stardream, and has a slight metallic shimmer.

Arts and crafts stores also sell X-Acto knives, steel rulers, scoring tools, cutting mats, adhesives, and everything else you might need for paper models.

New York Central Art Supply
62 Third Avenue, New York, NY 10003
Tel: 800 950 6111
www.nycentralart.com

Where Can I Learn More?

This section contains resources for paper, supplies, and techniques to help you create more kirigami. It also compiles all of the contributors' information—often their Web sites contain valuable tips as well, in addition to galleries of their work.

As you jump from one Web site to another, you'll see the community of paper artists firsthand. Members of this community are very supportive of one anothers' work, and will be interested to hear that you've enjoyed making their models or viewing their art. Don't hesitate to ask questions.

The Main Ingredient: Paper!

For kirigami and other lightweight paper-cutting projects, origami paper works well. However, thicker *washi* paper may not be easy to cut if folded more than three times. Origami is becoming so popular that many arts and crafts supply stores stock some selections; artists' supply stores often carry a larger range of specialty papers and cardstocks. Gift wrap is another excellent option for kirigami cutouts!

Cardstocks for pop-ups, origamic architecture, and a huge variety of specialty papers can be found on the Internet, through eBay, and at all of the stores listed here. The cardstock used for many of the

Kate's Paperie
561 Broadway, New York, NY 10012
Tel: 212 941 9816
www.katespaperie.com

Kinokuniya Bookstore
10 West 49th Street, New York, NY 10020
Tel: 212 765 7766
www.kinokuniya.com

Michaels Arts and Crafts Store
Locations throughout the United States
www.michaels.com

Aiko's Art Materials Import, Inc.
3347 North Clark Street, Chicago, IL 60657
Tel: 312 404 5600
www.aikosart.com

The Paper Tree
1743 Buchanan Mall, San Francisco, CA 94115
Tel: 415 921 7100
www.paper-tree.com

Bead and Wire Mobile Supplies

Small Parts, Inc.
Tubing: Tygon Microbore Tubing #TGY-030
Wire: Stainless Steel Wire Type 304, coiled #SWX-3035
www.smallparts.com

DOUBLE HEART KNOT, 2007, BY STEVEN R. WOODBURY

Societies, Guilds, and Groups

Many of the artists featured in this book are members of GAP—Guild of American Papercutters—a group stressing education and the furthering of the paper arts regardless of culture, tradition, or form.

www.papercutters.org

A directory of paper cutters and silhouette artists from around the world.

www.papercutters.info

Yahoo! Groups has artists and enthusiasts that share information, ideas, patterns, photos, and much, much more. Consider joining one of these groups: Kirigami-PaperCuts, scherenschnitte, and papercrafts.

groups.yahoo.com

Flickr is a photo-sharing Web site where many paper artists maintain galleries of new work.

www.flickr.com

René Bui maintains a Web site that is full of resources for artists and educators. But there's also a good selection of origamic architecture patterns for you to download, plus tips and tricks.

baudandbui.free.fr/plier/origamic.shtml

The Artists

Please visit the artists' Web sites or contact them to learn more about their work. The contributions they've made to this book represent just a small fraction of the talent given to us—and the world.

Joyce Aysta
www.liveyourdreamdesigns.com

Laura Badalucco
Kirigami—The Art of 3-Dimensional Papercutting
Sterling Publishing Co., Inc., 2001

Christiane Bettens
www.flickr.com/photos/melisande-origami

Lucrezia Bieler
www.bieler-beerli.com

Willem Boning
members.shaw.ca/woa/newhome.htm

Masahiro Chatani
www.japandesign.ne.jp/IAA/chatani/gallery

Jeff Cole
Kirigami Calendar
www.andrewsmcmeel.com

Béatrice Coron
www.beatricecoron.com

Jagoda Djuran
homepage.eircom.net/~jagoda/index.html

Bekah Gjerde
www.flickr.com/photos/lilzabubba

Eric Gjerde
www.origamitessellations.com

Beatriz Diaz Goodpasture
www.papelpicado.net

Archie Granot
www.archiegranot.com

George W. Hart
www.georgehart.com/slide-togethers/
slide-togethers.html

Chris Hankinson
www.popupcards.com

David Hathaway
www.dhathaway.freeserve.co.uk/origami/
origamic_arch.htm

Cindy Higham
www.allseasonsnowflakes.com

Mark Hiner
www.markhiner.co.uk

Joyce Hwang
www.stonebridge.com

Paul Jackson
www.origami-artist.com

Magdalena Jonikas
www.geocities.com/origamic_architecture

Pat Kelley
www.papersnowflakes.com

Anna Kronick
www.kronickart.com

Kathy Monahan
joeandkathy@charter.net

Keiko Nakazawa
www.neo-di.com/KAI/english/indexE.html

Chris K. Palmer
www.shadowfolds.com/polarlights

Liz Peterson
perspicacious.org

Ramin Razani
officinacrea.it
Kirigami Faszinierende Grußkarten
www.droemer-knaur.de

Fernando Sierra
www.ambientesluar.com

Ingrid Siliakus
members.chello.nl/rebran
www.ingrid-siliakus.exto.org

Gerlof Smit
www.gerlofsmit.com

Jen Stark
www.jenstark.com

Tatyana Stolyarova
r-i-w.tomsk.ru/pop-up/index.htm
www.flickr.com/photos/tekuila

Richard Sweeney
www.richardsweeney.co.uk

Florence Temko
www.bloominxpressions.com/origami.htm

Peter Visser
Iceberg Paper Models
www.icebergbouwplaten.nl

Steven R. Woodbury
Founding member of the Guild of American
Papercutters and first President

Jiacai Yin
www.sino-arts.com/papercutG.html

Abbey Elinon Yu
obie_wan_kenabbey_is@yahoo.com.au

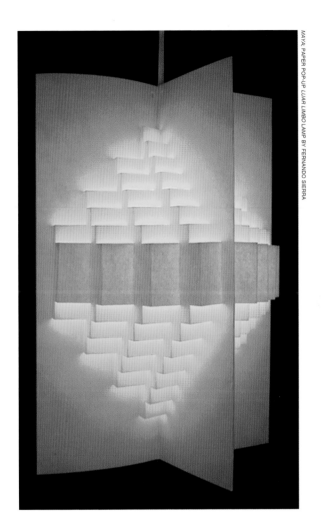

Fernando Sierra is an industrial designer who has developed a range of paper and polypropylene lamps called Luar. "Luar is a Portuguese word referring to the ambience generated under the moonlight." Sierra illuminates the imagination with these lamps, which come in a wide variety of styles all featuring simple geometric shapes.

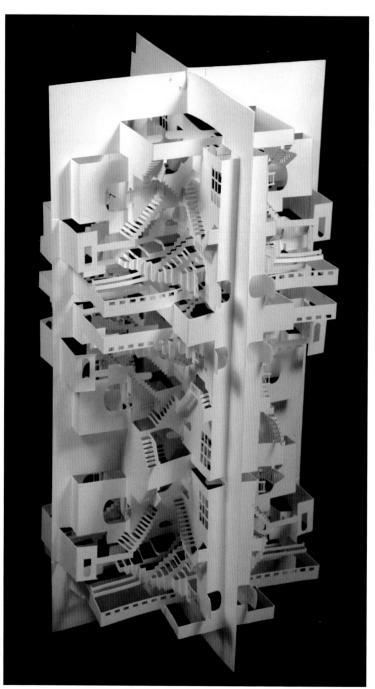

Joyce Aysta used to be a costume designer in Hollywood before she turned her attention to the art of kirigami, combining her cutting skills and her love of the architecture in Southern California. "I begin by drawing on my computer, then cut and fold a sample by hand, and contemplate the design. My finished designs are cut using two laser cutters." She estimates she can cut and fold 200 to 300 cards per day! Aysta lives and works in Los Angeles.

When she discovered paper architecture, Ingrid Siliakus was instantly fascinated by the ingenuity of the designs, and the beauty they radiated. "To design a pattern from scratch, the artist needs the skills of an architect ... then, with the patience and precision of a surgeon, it can become a three-dimensional wonder in paper." Her specialty is cards that recreate buildings by master architects such as H. P. Berlage and Antoni Gaudí, as well as intricate, abstract sculptures inspired by the works of M. C. Escher. Siliakus lives and works in Amsterdam.

Jeff Rutzky's report card in kindergarten stated that he "works well with paper and scissors." Paper crafts have been a passion throughout his life, and in his adulthood, he has integrated them with his desktop publishing skills to create unique works of art.

Recently, Jeff discovered the wonders of Graphtec's Craft ROBO—a computer-controlled cutting machine for paper, card-stocks, and lightweight plastics. Smaller than a breadbox, this amazing "new toy" helped create many of the models shown in this book. He hopes it will save him from X-Acto cuts and wrist fatigue.

Jeff is also the author and designer of *TearPlanes*, *Jewelgami*, and *Bugagami*—origami books that feature unique and beautiful micro-perforated paper with each page.

Jeff works as an author, graphic designer, and artist in New York City.